Writing
Beyond Race

Writing
Beyond Race

LIVING THEORY
AND PRACTICE

bell hooks

Routledge
Taylor & Francis Group

NEW YORK AND LONDON

Chapter 11 appeared originally as "A Community of Care" in *Belonging*, hooks (2009): 224–230. © 2009 Taylor & Francis.

A version of Chapter 8 appeared on *Mindful.org* as "Surrendered to Love." © 2011 bell hooks

First published 2013
by Routledge
711 Third Avenue, New York, NY 10017

Simultaneously published in the UK
by Routledge
2 Park Square, Milton Park, Abingdon, Oxon OX14 4RN

Routledge is an imprint of the Taylor & Francis Group, an informa business

© 2013 Taylor & Francis

The right of bell hooks to be identified as author of this work has been asserted by him/her in accordance with sections 77 and 78 of the Copyright, Designs and Patents Act 1988.

Library of Congress Cataloging in Publication Data

hooks, bell.
  Writing beyond race : living theory and practice/bell hooks. — 1st ed.
    p. cm.
  1. Racism—United States—History. 2. United States—Race relations—History. I. Title.
  E184.A1H654 2013
  305.800973—dc23   2012014263

ISBN: 978-0-415-53914-2 (hbk)
ISBN: 978-0-415-53915-9 (pbk)
ISBN: 978-0-203-10849-9 (ebk)

Typeset in BemboStd
by Apex CoVantage

Printed and bound in the United States of America by Sheridan Books, Inc. (a Sheridan Group Company)

for James Hillman
beloved comrade

Contents

1

Introduction

In recent years my work has focused on the role of love in ending domination. Contemplating the factors that lead people to struggle for justice and strive to build community has led me to think critically about the place of love. Whether the issue is ending racism, sexism, homophobia, or class elitism, when I interview folks about what leads them to overcome dominator thinking and action they invariably speak about love, about learning acceptance of difference from someone they care about. They talk about being rigorously challenged by the longing to connect and join with someone who is either radically different or holds beliefs and opinions so unlike their own as to be a source of estrangement and conflict, so much so that only sustained, caring, critical vigilance can ensure continued contact. For many of these individuals it is active involvement with movements to end domination that has pushed them in the direction of critical thinking and change.

When feminist theory and cultural criticism privileged ending domination, challenging all of us to move beyond the barriers created by race, gender, class, sexuality, and/or religious differences, for a time at least, it appeared that we would be entering a brave new world where differences could be understood and embraced, where we would all seek to learn from the "other," whomever that other might be. All the theories of border crossing, of finding a way to "get a bit of the other," did not fundamentally change the nature of dominator culture. Our theory was far more progressive and inclusive in its vision than our everyday life practice. In our everyday lives all of us confront barriers to communication—divisive hierarchies that make joining together difficult, if not impossible. Many of us found that it was easier to name the problem and to deconstruct it, and yet it was hard to create theories that would help us build community, help us border cross with the intention of truly remaining connected in a space of difference long enough to be transformed.

Public discourses about race and gender did create new ways of thinking and knowing. Talking about class and the various ways class differences separate groups has been much harder. Class standing and status tend frequently to link us more intimately to the dominant economic system and its concomitant hierarchies. For example: it is much more likely that a white person will bond with a black person when the two share a common class lifestyle. It is less likely that a materially prosperous person will establish a mutual bond with someone who is poor and indigent. One of the most difficult and delicate subjects to discuss among African Americans is the reality of class differences and of class difference among us. The central position race has occupied in our political discourse has often obscured the way in which class differences disrupt notions of racial unity. And yet, today, class differences coupled with racial integration have created a cultural context where the very meaning of blackness and its impact on our lives differs greatly among black people. There is no longer a common notion of shared black identity.

In other words, a sense of shared identity is no longer a platform that can draw folks together in meaningful solidarity. Along with class, gender issues and feminist awareness have served to place black folks in different camps, creating conflicts that can only be resolved through education for critical consciousness. There is also the reality of changing religious practices. There was a time in our nation when it was just assumed that every black person was a Christian or at least coming from a Christian background. This is simply no longer the case. Black children today have diverse religious practices. Some are raised in Muslim and Buddhist traditions with no understanding of Christian beliefs. And more young black people than ever before choose no religious practice at all. Hence the shared theological language that once served as a basis of communication and bonding can no longer be assumed.

Many of these changes to the nature of black identity are a direct consequence of racial integration. Prior to racial integration most educated black folks, especially those with higher degrees, were educated within a similar segregated pedagogical context and were more than likely to have a shared mindset. It is political movement that has allowed greater class mobility, making it possible for materially prosperous black folks to leave historically black communities and live elsewhere. The opening up of educational possibilities has led to the formation of classes of black individuals with radically different educational backgrounds, diverse perspectives and values, as well as varied political leanings. Consequently, bonding between black folks (even within families where there are not major class differences) has become more difficult.

Significantly, despite class differences, as a group, white people (whether consciously or unconsciously) maintain some degree of bonding despite diversities of standpoint. White supremacist thinking continues to be the invisible and visible glue that keeps white folks connected irrespective of many other differences. Politically, white supremacist thinking was created to serve this purpose. Imprinted on the consciousness of every white child at birth, reinforced by the culture, white supremacist thinking tends to function unconsciously. This is the primary reason it is so difficult to challenge and change.

In order to talk openly and honestly about race in the United States it is helpful to begin with the understanding that it is white supremacist thinking and practice that has been the political foundation undergirding all systems of domination based on skin color and ethnicity. When describing the political system that we live within here in the United States, more often than not, I use the complicated phrase *imperialist white supremacist capitalist patriarchy.* This phrase is useful precisely because it does not prioritize one system over another but rather offers us a way to think about the interlocking systems that work together to uphold and maintain cultures of domination.

However, in talking and writing about these systems for more than thirty years, I have found that most citizens of the United States resist the notion that ours is a nation founded and colonized on a foundation of white supremacist thought and action. And yet, as a nation we have always had a public discourse about race and racism. And, when leaders of our nation have called for a national dialogue on these issues, there has been little resistance. The United States was colonized and founded by a white supremacist politics that necessitated endless thinking, writing, and discussion about race. White folks from all places and classes, speaking all manner of languages, migrated here in the hopes of creating a better, more prosperous, freer life for themselves. They, for the most part, collectively, accepted a national identity based on the fictions of race and racism created by white supremacist thought and action. Bonding on the basis of shared whiteness provides the foundation for a sense of shared meaning, values, and purpose. With the battle cry of preserving whiteness, imperialist colonization became the belief system that supported the mass murder of indigenous natives, the blatant stealing of their lands, and the creation of segregated reservations. Despite the presence of African individuals who came to the so-called new world before Columbus—as documented in Ivan Van Sertima's seminal work *They Came Before Columbus*—white supremacist thinking and action condoned the enslavement of black Africans, supporting their brutal exploitation and oppression.

Living as they did in close proximity with enslaved black folks, relying on them to serve obediently and subserviently, white dominators needed a psychological mode of colonization that would keep everyone in check, that would teach everyone their place in the race-based hierarchy that is the aim of white supremacist thinking and practice. At this point, notions of white supremacy were fluid and constantly changing to meet the needs of dominating white colonizers. When white supremacist logic decreed that all black folks were diseased and unclean, that train of thought then had to be shifted a bit to leave just enough room for it to be deemed acceptable for some black folks to cook for white owners and to care for their children. When white supremacist logic decreed that the brains of black folks were smaller than those of whites, thus rendering them intellectually inferior, and then well-educated black genius asserted itself, there had to be space made within the theory of white superiority for exceptions. Clearly, one of the awesome aspects of white supremacist logic has been its fluidity, its ability to adjust and change according to need and circumstance.

Throughout the nineteenth and early twentieth century, dialogues about white supremacy were common. Few, if any, white folks would have found it odd for there to be silence on the subject. Yet talk of white supremacy in our society is deemed not only taboo, but also irrelevant. When addressed openly there is always a listener eager to insist that the term *white supremacy* has little meaning in the contemporary United States, that it is too harsh a reality to be relevant to discussions of race and racism.

When I speak with audiences about imperialist white supremacist capitalist patriarchy, the one piece of these interlocking political systems that individuals most resist acknowledging is white supremacy. And yet if we cannot as a culture accept the way white supremacist thinking and practice informs some aspect of our lives irrespective of skin color, then we will never move beyond race. Unlike race and racism, which does not overtly harm masses of folk in ways that causes direct damage, white supremacy is the covert ideology that is the silent cause of harm and trauma. Think of the black children, both rich and poor, who watch long hours of television that imprints their young minds with the notion that white is good and black is bad. All over the United States, parents who assume they have taught their families to be actively anti-racist are shocked when they discover that their children harbor intense anti-black feelings. This is just one example. Another example might be the interracial couple in which the white individual proclaims their undying love for a black partner but then later in conversation talks about their belief that black people are intellectually inferior. This is not an expression of conventional racial prejudice. It does however remind us that one can be intimate with black folks, claim even to love us, and yet still hold white supremacist attitudes about the nature of black identity.

Thinking about white supremacy as the foundation of race and racism is crucial because it allows us to see beyond skin color. It allows us to look at all the myriad ways our daily actions can be imbued by white supremacist thinking no matter our race. Certainly, race and racism will never become unimportant if we cannot recognize the need to consistently challenge white supremacy. When cultural studies emerged as a context where the issue of whiteness and white privilege could be studied and theorized, it appeared that a new way of thinking and talking about race was emerging. Even though scholars wrote much about white privilege, they did not always endeavor to show the link between underlying notions of white supremacy and white privilege. Overracializing whiteness then made it seem as though white skin and the privileges that it allows were the primary issues, and not the white supremacist ways of thinking and acting that are expressed by folks of all skin colors. It may very well be that the re-centering of whiteness has helped silence the necessary theories and practice that are needed if we are as a nation to truly learn how to be rid of racism.

Similarly, feminist focus on gender, which initially provided amazing insights into the nature of patriarchy and gave hope to those struggling to bring sexist exploitation and domination to an end, was soon usurped by a depoliticized focus on gender. We now have much published work that looks at race and gender but not from a standpoint that is feminist or anti-racist. This is a deeply disturbing trend. Among those of us who have spent our lifetimes critically thinking and writing about ways to transform both our individual lives and our society so that systems of domination can be challenged and changed, there is a growing mood of frustration and despair. We feel we are constantly deconstructing and laying the groundwork for alternatives without making the interventions in how folks live daily that are needed if our society is to be utterly changed.

Significantly, in the last ten years, there have been so many cutbacks at colleges and universities that the longed for diversity of faculty and staff not only is not happening, it is unlikely to ever happen. At many institutions, when jobs appear, conventional hierarchies of race and gender fall back into place. This reminds many critical thinkers of how important it is to encourage everyone to learn new points of view, to engage in unbiased thinking and teaching. The burden of learning new points of view should not have been placed solely on the shoulders of people of color. Intervention that helps us all better understand the way interlocking systems of domination work together is consistently needed.

The motley collection of essays in *Writing Beyond Race* all emerge from my efforts to look at the ways race, gender, and class are written and talked about today. After the feminist and cultural studies heyday, where for a time so much new ground was broken and radical discussions of non-biased standpoints were made prominent, these discourses are suddenly no longer at the forefront of our consciousness. While the subjects of race, gender, and class are still talked about, they are more and more divorced from discussions of ending biases in standpoint, and so they risk becoming mere topics of inquiry with no relation to transformative learning or practical change.

In these essays I focus attention on issues of accountability, standpoint, and white supremacy. Specifically, I examine those cultural productions which give the surface appearance of addressing topics of race, gender, and class, while merely reinscribing ideologies of domination. Not wanting to simply paint a bleak picture of where things stand, I address in several essays what allows us to bond across differences, placing emphasis on patterns of positive change. Most importantly, I am attempting to think and write beyond the boundaries which keep us all overracialized. To find a way to move beyond race is not only the goal of critical thinking, it is the only path to emotional longevity, the only true path to liberation.

2

Racism:
Naming What Hurts

At a time in our nation when more folk than ever before are daring to "talk" race, many of us who have been speaking and writing on the subject for years are oddly silent. Some of us do not want to be heard sharing that they "are sick and tired of talking about race." Still other folks wonder what good does all the talking do when so much remains the same, when our nation's acceptable discourses of race are inextricably tied to the normalized practices of racism and white supremacy. Contrary to the popular assumption that folks find it difficult to talk about race, the truth of the matter is that most folks talk about race all the time, that one of the ways everyday racism has made its imprint on the lives of black people/people of color has been through the many overheard comments that are overt expressions of hate speech. All around us, negative stereotypes can be heard, overt racist epitaphs abound. The election of a black male president has simply brought these stereotypes out of the closet and made them more public. Making racist comments has become more acceptable for everyone, especially when those comments occur in an atmosphere where all around us we hear that racism no longer exists.

When folks insist that racism is gone, what they usually mean is that black people/people of color have gained enough civil rights through antidiscrimination laws and practices that we are no longer subjected to constant racial terrorism or overt brutal punishments based on race. The great paradox of our nation's relationship to race is that if you were to go door to door and ask every white person if racial prejudice is still a problem most folks would say yes. Then if you were to ask them if this prejudice adversely effects black folks more than other groups, most folks would probably say no. And if the conversation continued, they may even proclaim that there is very little anti-black prejudice. It is not that your average white American citizens do not understand that racism is alive and well, it is simply that they believe it is no longer a meaningful threat to anyone's well-being. Along with this sentiment (which is not based on facts or study), a huge majority of white folks simply believe that black folks have received unearned gains and rewards and that this perceived reality of being given many breaks evens the score and cancels out any racial injustice past and present. Indeed, how often across class boundaries do individual black folk hear from other groups, especially white folks, say that "they are sick and tired of hearing black folks complain about racism, that they can't stand the whining, that black folks are their own worst enemies."

Imagine a scenario where you are the lone black female working in a predominately white office, and at meetings and at lunch your colleagues talk about and joke about lazy "niggahs." When you go to the boss and talk about diversity training, about the need for everyone to understand hate speech, you are told you are misreading the situation, that you are being too sensitive, that folks are just having fun. No one listens when you tell them that when folks say the "n" word in a context where they are not being actively anti-racist that it triggers memories of trauma and fear. Time and time again you confront them and even when they admit that they can understand why you do not find it amusing, they tell you they are talking about the "bad" black people when they make racist comments, "not good black people." Again and again they assure you they mean no harm. This scenario is a common one experienced probably by every black person/person of color who has or is working in an a work space where few, if any, white workers have unlearned racism.

When these incidents happen to all people of color and especially black people, it simply reinforces our conviction that we can never be free of racism, that we are never safe. Unaware white folks who have not chosen to unlearn racism, who in most areas of their lives are generally decent and well-intentioned, have no idea the extent to which black people, across class, live with constant anxiety and/or fear that we will be the innocent targets of random racist assault. Of course, the white folks who are openly committed to maintaining white supremacism at all costs boast of their efforts to humiliate, shame, and terrorize every person of color they encounter. Nowadays, many black people/people of color have accepted that living with racism is just an unchanging fact of life. But, by passively accepting racism and believing it cannot be changed, we unwittingly collude with all the unenlightened racist white folks who embrace white supremacist thought and action.

Again and again visionary thinkers on the subject of race encourage us to confront directly and honestly the way in which white supremacist ideology informs the lives of everyone in our nation to a greater or lesser degree. We can move beyond the us/them binaries that usually surface in most discussions of race and racism if we focus on the ways in which white supremacist thought is a foundational belief system in this nation. White supremacist thinking informs the consciousness of everyone irrespective of skin color.

In more recent years cultural critics focusing on color caste hierarchies among black people/people of color, which deem fairer skinned people to be more beautiful than their darker skinned counterparts, remind everyone that this way of thinking and acting is a startling indication of how deeply engrained white supremacist aesthetics constantly shape identity and behavior. No white dominating authority has to be present for these practices of white supremacy to impinge on the lives of black people. In the daily lives of black folk/people of color, white supremacist thought and action permeate diverse cultures making it clear that the problem of racism is not solely a function of the actions of white folk. If everyone in our society could face that white supremacist thinking is the underlying belief system informing nearly every aspect of this nation's culture and habits of daily life, then all our discussions of race and racism would be based on a foundation of concrete reality. Everyone could move away from the us/them dichotomies which promote blame and prevent us all from assuming accountability for challenging and changing white supremacy. Unless we make a conscious effort to change thought and action by honestly naming all the myriad ways white supremacy impinges on daily life then we cannot shift from a politics of hate and create a new foundation based on a revolution of love.

A primary reason this nation refuses to offer an adequate political language to define racial politics lies with the insistence that this is the most democratic nation in the world, a place where freedom and justice for all is possible. Citizens of the United States had no difficulty naming the politics of white supremacy in South Africa because the extreme racial segregation and the concomitant violence deployed to protect the system of apartheid was overt and consciously supported by government and law makers. Here in the United States most folks want to believe that the United States has never had and does not currently have a politics of race based on the support and maintenance of racial apartheid.

Yet all children in this nation are inundated from birth on into adulthood with white supremacist thinking and practice. And it is more insidious because it is often a hidden socialization. The most powerful covert teacher of white supremacy is mass media. Even parents who strive to teach their children to be anti-racist find they must be constantly vigilant as white supremacist attitudes and beliefs come from so many different sources. This became evident to Kathleen and James McGinnis, authors of the helpful and insightful book *Parenting for Peace and Justice,* when they became a more racially diverse family. Already the parents of two white boys, they adopted a brown-skinned Native American girl. When she was only one year old her five-year-old brother wanted to know, "Mommy, when Theresa grows up will she kill us?" As they pondered where this idea came from they looked at the cultural images coming from mass media.

Having worked consciously to create an anti-racist household, they realized their children were still being inundated by white supremacist thinking in school: "It was a startling indication to us of how deeply ingrained stereotypes, misconceptions, and fears can be, even at a very early age. Tommy, who at the time did not know any Indian people besides Theresa, had a very clear and very negative idea about what Indians do to people." In this case, as in all cases where very young children express racialized fear or hatred, there is an imprinting incident. While there is discussion of white children's negative imprinting around race, it is equally true that black children and other children of color may have similar imprints that come from either images they have seen or stories they hear. Most folks have heard about the doll study, where black children choose white dolls over dolls who look like themselves because they have learned white is better. There are even studies of negative racial imprinting which have looked at the messages about visual difference sent to babies, which indicate that white parents who see a person of color and respond by holding the baby tighter thereby transmit non-verbally that darker skinned people are to be feared. It seems likely that were studies showing black and brown parents to act in a similar way when in close proximity to a white person the imprinting experience might be the same.

As long as this nation absolutely refuses to accurately name white supremacy then the roots of racism will remain strong. Ironically, even though feminist theory and cultural criticism have led to the study of whiteness and white privilege, very little of this work addresses the issue of white supremacy. When we engage a discourse that focuses on white supremacy it enables us to see ways individuals who gain no "privilege" by allegiance to white supremacist thought and action collude in the perpetuation and maintenance of this system. Here is another common racialized scenario involving children: a white girl child born blonde is constantly told by everyone she comes into contact with how beautiful she is and therefore worthy of more attention and regard than those considered less attractive. However, as the child ages, her hair begins to darken and as a consequence she is no longer the recipient of the hyper-regard shown to her as a blonde. Increasingly, she feels invisible; in some cases she would rather die than not continue her life as a blonde. Like her darker counterpart who seeks to lighten her skin with toxic bleaching cleaners, this little girl has learned that in a white supremacist context lighter is always better.

In her book *It's The Little Things: Everyday Interactions That Anger, Annoy, and Divide the Races,* African American journalist Lena Williams tells the story of a high-powered black friend who had purchased a house where the kitchen floor was decorated with old movie posters. Living with these images she was surprised when her four-year-old daughter announced: "Mommy, I don't want to be black…Nobody likes black people!" Her evidence of this included the fact that there were no images of black folks in the movie posters. Her mother was astonished by this: "I hadn't noticed that only white people were in the posters, but here was my four-year-old child—whose mommy was a lawyer and daddy a doctor—getting this message." Williams includes this story in a chapter that discusses the way all the images that surround us, even though they may appear to be benign, often reveal the degree to which our lives are governed by an underlying ethic of white supremacy.

In the growing body of critical work on whiteness there is more writing than ever before about race and aesthetics. Work that looks at the way in which the politics of white supremacy creates an aesthetic where the color and texture of hair determines value, setting standards where lighter, straighter, and longer hair equates with beauty and desirability. New work on hair like the book *Big Hair* informs us that only a small population of white people in the United States are born blonde and that the sad reality is that personal aesthetics rooted in white supremacist thinking lead large numbers of white females to dye their hair blonde from their teens on into adulthood. Nowadays there are segregated hair salons that specifically cater to white females desiring to be always and only blonde. Browsing any contemporary fashion magazine one sees that blondes predominate; they set the standards for what is deemed truly beautiful. While there is an ongoing discussion about the way in which white supremacist–based color caste systems create trauma in black lives, there is little discussion of the way in which these same standards create distress and trauma for white folks. Moviegoers can see a film like Chris Rock's *Good Hair* and marvel at the torture and painful self-mutilation black females undergo to look "white" but do not document the torture white females face when they strive to acquire the right really white look. Even though everyone in this society is inundated with white supremacist aesthetics and will remain its victim unless we consciously choose against it, we are still encouraged to consider the issue of race as primarily a matter of black and white.

Certainly it serves the interest of dominator culture to promote a shallow understanding of race politics that consistently makes it appear that the issues of race in the United States solely rest on the status of darker skinned people. It may well be that the growing Hispanic population (which too is invested heavily in white supremacist aesthetics) will help push the discourse of race past issues of black and white and toward the issue of white supremacist thought and action. Every black person who talks about race has an experience where they have been interrogated about their focus on issues of black and white. Rarely does a person of color who is non-black acknowledge that the most intense forms of racial assault and discrimination in our nation have been directed primarily at black people. Professing this understanding and allegiance with black anti-racist struggles would do more to affirm challenges to white supremacy than competing for the status of who will receive more attention. The fact is when black people receive that greater attention from the dominant white society it is usually negative.

Despite gains in civil rights a huge majority of white Americans and some non-black people of color continue to believe that black people are less intelligent, full of rage, and more likely to express anger with violence than all other groups. Even though negative racist stereotypes about Asian identities abound, there is no overwhelming consensus on the part of white Americans that they are incapable of intelligent rational thought. It is troubling that so many of the hateful negative stereotypes the dominant culture uses to characterize black identity are endorsed by non-black people of color. Their endorsement is an expression of collusion and solidarity with white supremacist thought and action. If all people of color and even our white allies in struggle were decolonizing their minds, challenging and changing white supremacy, they could see value in identification with blackness rather than feeling there must always be competition over who will receive the most attention from white folks. They would see clearly that the system of domination that remains oppressive and exploitative is ever ready to recruit and train as many black, brown, red, and yellow people as are needed to maintain the status quo.

A thorough understanding of the complex dynamic of white supremacist thought and action would provide all citizens with a way to understand why this nation can elect a black man to be its leader and yet resist any system-wide efforts, both public and private, to challenge and change racial inequality. From the moment he entered the oval office, Obama's actions have been continually subject to policing to ensure he does act in any way that brings particular benefits to African American citizens. Sadly, even though there have been wonderful advances in anti-discrimination–based civil rights laws and public agendas, there has been no profound effort to destroy the roots of racism. Instead we live in a society that claims via our government and public policy to condemn racial discrimination even as imperialist white supremacist capitalist patriarchy shapes our politics and culture.

Even though we have a racially integrated workforce, however relative that may be, one wherein white folks and folks of color share common ground, working together without overt strife, individuals rarely meet outside the workforce and a veneer of peace is the norm. White folks and people of color continue to negatively assess one another even though their actual lived experience of interracial connection should provide cause for them to interrogate false beliefs and assumptions. One of the sad ironies of racism in the United States is that so many black people/people of color unwittingly collude in the perpetuation of white supremacy while simultaneously denouncing racism and actively speaking out against racial injustice.

Most black people/people of color rarely raise the issue of white supremacy even though the values it promotes are internalized by almost everyone. Throughout the nation's history most racialized civil rights struggle has focused on the exploitation and oppression of black people by whites. And even though more militant anti-racist struggle, like the movement for black power, called attention to internalized racism, this awareness did not become the basis for a national restructuring of anti-racist political struggle. Instead, the issues that have been raised by a focus on internalized racism (color caste hierarchies, low self-esteem, self-hatred, etc.) came to be regarded as more personal, and therefore more psychological and not truly political. During much of the militant black power movement anger and rage were the emotions anti-racist advocates fixated on as essential catalysts for liberation struggle. That highlighting of anger as a basis for resistance was far more appealing as an organizing tool than the issue of internalized racism or even a focus on self-determination.

Certainly, while Malcolm X was the black power advocate who most called attention to internalized racism, his early focus on rage as a catalyst for protest was deemed more important. Joe Wood's essay "Malcolm X and the New Blackness," included in the anthology he edited, *Malcolm X: In Our Own Image,* examines the call for a true black spirit. That spirit, he explained, was "a 'true' Black spirit, meaning 'militant,' 'proud,' 'angry.'" Writing about the significance of the dead leader as an iconic figure, Wood asserts: "Malcolm's icon has consequently come to signify the 'truest' distillation of this Black spirit and therefore the best product to validate and express 'real' Black anger: anger about the way Black people have been treated everywhere we are Black, anger about the way we are now treated in America…Malcolm's icon proclaims anger so forcefully it even attracts angry non–African Americans; fellow travelers, hangers-on, and other assorted buyers purchase Malcolm, too." Wood's collection was published in 1992 and largely focused on the way in which the commodification of Malcolm as a celebrity had served to deflect attention away from his radical politics, his call for global confrontation of white supremacy. And it was especially Malcolm's demand that black folks actively change our consciousness and divest of internalized white supremacy that has no longer been given much attention.

More than other black leaders Malcolm X worked to call attention to black folks' passive acceptance of white supremacy. His contemporary "fans" tend to focus on the angry icon image and not on his consistent call for the development of critical thinking and critical consciousness—a call which he named "psychic conversion." He insisted that black folks work on decolonizing the mind, consciously taking steps to unlearn white supremacist thinking. In his essay "Malcolm X and Black Rage," philosopher Cornel West explains: "In other words, Malcolm X crystallized sharply the relation of Black affirmation of self, Black desire for freedom, Black rage against American society…. Black psychic conversion—the decolonization of the mind, body and soul that strips white-supremacist lies of their authority, legitimacy and efficacy—begins with a bold and defiant rejection of Black degradation, and is sustained by urgent efforts to expand those spaces where

Black humanity is affirmed." Yet despite Malcolm's powerful leadership, his focus on decolonizing the mind did not have as much impact as his focus on using anger and rage to denounce white privilege.

Those individual black folks concerned with striving for self-determination who embraced the notion that this process would necessarily begin with the throwing off of the shackles of internalized racism and building a foundation for healthy self-esteem did not interest the racist white world or white media. Black folks expressing rage and talking about hating whitey—now that was worthy of media attention. And of course white folks liked hearing about white power and white privilege: it confirmed that the system they believed in was working. As black freedom struggle gained attention, the emphasis was no longer on internalized racism. White supremacy was rarely mentioned. Black leaders began to equate gaining freedom solely with gaining economic power, with getting what it was assumed white folks had.

Malcolm X's call for decolonization, for "changing our minds and hearts" and looking at each other with "new eyes," had long been forgotten. Those folks who pushed for black self-determination, daring to focus on the psychological health of black folks, represented the most powerful threat to white supremacist power. That threat could be rendered harmless by simply deflecting attention away from anyone who focused on both the trauma black folks experienced as victims of ongoing racial assault and the process by which those wounds could be healed. Concurrently, as black and white civil rights activists, whether conservative or militant, all focused more on achieving economic parity as the best way to uplift the black race, the psychological work of unlearning white supremacist thinking, of challenging and changing those aspects of life that support the system, as well as the struggle to build foundations for healthy self-esteem, did not remain a central agenda of black liberation struggle.

Increasingly the old notion that racism had not diminished black spirit began to gain new ground, as did the insistence that black people had not been victimized by racialized trauma but instead had transcended the dehumanization and degradation of slavery, reconstruction, and the long hard years of legal apartheid. Equating freedom with economic power made it possible for black folks to ignore the extent to which class privilege did not mean that individuals do not suffer the negative psychological impacts of racism and white supremacy. Significantly, as black poverty has intensified, despite more and more black people entering the ranks of the materially privileged, there is just as much contemporary equation of economic privilege with freedom. The notion that making money and being materially privileged automatically leads to healthier self-esteem is widespread. When super-wealthy black individuals, like Michael Jackson, reveal that they suffer from low self-esteem and self-hatred, their experience is seen as aberrant; it is never viewed as part of a collective trauma. And even when Jackson re-evaluated through music his struggle to accept blackness, it certainly did not lead to a collective call that black people renew the struggle to challenge and change white supremacy in black life. No one talked about cognitive restructuring of the mind so as to create a healthy social context for the self-development and growth of black folks, specifically black children. Then and now, these issues were seen as matters that are personal and private—not political.

Of course, it is obvious that white supremacists would promote ignoring psychological decolonization in favor of a focus on economics. Sharing a small bit of the economic pie has not undermined imperialist white supremacist capitalist patriarchy. Quite the opposite has occurred. The more individual black folk have gained power and status within the existing social structure, the less concerned they've been with dismantling that social structure. In the 1980s and 1990s, when many discriminatory practices were no longer legitimized by public policy and racial integration opened avenues in the workforce that were once utterly closed, a significant number of black people gained greater economic privilege. Of course, what is significant is that these material gains had little impact on wounded psyches damaged by internalized racism.

Clearly, as black people/people of color seek to gain status and power within the existing dominator culture, colluding with white supremacy perversely became and becomes an asset; it makes it easier to assimilate into mainstream culture. It creates a common ground that allows skin color difference to mean little. Right now in the popular cartoon sitcom *The Boondocks* (created by black artist Aaron McGruder), there is a black character who openly and vigorously espouses white supremacist thinking. And while many viewers like to consider this a satiric portrait, he is actually not portrayed ironically. Even though assuming the values of white supremacy provides a veneer of self-acceptance and may prepare all people of color to achieve better material success in existing social structures, psychic harm is the daily toxic hazard that is not confronted, and when denied, it undermines physical and psychological well-being.

When the diseases that most impact on the bodies of black people are examined, it is evident that they are all caused in some way by stress. And it is equally evident that class privilege for black folks does not necessarily lead to better health. In a 2009 article from *Miller-McCune*, "Racism's Hidden Toll," writer Ryan Blitstein begins his comments by stating: "The long-term stress of living in a white-dominated society 'weathers' blacks, making them age faster than their white counterparts." His article highlights the research of a white female academic, Arline Geronimus, who has made a career of studying this phenomenon. Of course, black folks have known for years that the traumatic experiences caused by facing racist assault and/or the chronic stress of coping with everyday racism causes health problems, but when an enlightened white person shares this news, folks appear more willing to listen. As Geronimus progressed in her research, "the more she read, the more she began to agree with the radical notion that it wasn't anything inherent to their race that made black people sick—it was being black in a racist society." Furthermore, Blitstein explains: "The phrase 'racism kills' would be a vast oversimplification of Geronimus' ideas, but the way she describes it, racism is a fundamental cause of health disparities." Notably, when the term *racism* is used, it continues to evoke for most folks notions of overt assaults and discrimination. Using the term *white supremacy* allows for the uncovering and exposure of all the covert and insidious ways that coping with trauma and stress may diminish one's chances of being in good health.

In his insightful book *Emotional Longevity: What Really Determines How Long You Live,* Norman B. Anderson explains: "Not only do race and ethnicity shape many of our life experiences, they can be powerful predictors of longevity. Although many differences in health and longevity are evident between racial and ethnic groups, perhaps the most striking example is the health difference between blacks and whites. Compared to whites, blacks suffer higher death rates from nearly every illness, including heart disease, cancer, diabetes, cirrhosis of the liver, and HIV/AIDS, as well as from homicide." Anderson does allow for the reality that socioeconomics impacts health, but research shows that it is not the sole or even the major determining factor. For example, he calls attention to the fact that black poor folk have higher death rates than white poor folks.

While many black people who have material success also have better access to health care, working in the predominately white (and ipso facto white supremacist) work environment causes tremendous stress. And this stress undermines the immune system. Of course, there is little work documenting the physical and psychological health of super-rich, rich, and just plain upper-class black folks. In more recent years just making it to millionaire status may place one in the ranks of black folks deemed successful and worthy of being emulated. Only recently has there been more work on matters directly affecting the health of all black people. Individual black people who have gained greater economic power and status (like Oprah Winfrey, who has great wealth) are seen as role models even if they daily reveal that they are unable to throw off the shackles imprisoning their minds. Indeed, like their less wealthy underprivileged counterparts, they exercise "split mind," living lives where there is often no congruency between what they think, say, and do.

The pursuit of liberal individualism sanctioned by imperialist white supremacist capitalist patriarchy has allowed all collective calls for black self-determination to be co-opted by the hunger to participate as pseudo equals in the existing dominator culture. Amiri Baraka reminds us of this in his important essay "Malcolm as Ideology," stating that "Malcolm's fundamental ideological stance to white supremacy is opposition and an attempt to destroy it." However, as black male leaders in the black power movement began to equate black liberation with the formation of a strong black patriarchy, as has already been stated, issues of psychological trauma faded into the background and the focus was on money and masculinity.

From a contemporary vantage point, it is easy to look back and see that white supremacist capitalist patriarchy has never afforded black people/people of color equal access to economic development and economic privilege. And it makes perfect sense that it is the materially privileged upper- and middle-class black folks who have thrived within this system and that masses of black people continue to struggle to make ends meet. The reality that individual black folks have made tremendous economic gains does not correlate to constructive psychic convergences where decolonizing the mind lays a groundwork for healthy self-actualization. That black people spent more than forty million dollars in the late nineties on skin-lightening creams (that number is probably even more astronomical today) reveals the deeply engrained shame many blacks feel about their skin color. The money spent on hair products that straighten kinky locks is even more outrageous. All these cultural and aesthetic practices are rooted in white supremacist aesthetics that continue to set the standards for what is deemed beautiful and desirable.

Among people of color, black folks, more so than other groups, spend huge sums of money on mass media that demeans and diminishes black identity. Collective black self-esteem is so degraded that negative images (especially violent ones) are what is seen as pleasurable and entertaining. When slavery ended and on into the years of Jim Crow, black folks vigilantly protested the reproduction of colonizing images. But once individual black folks discovered they could acquire wealth by creating and producing these images, there has been little or no collective effort to protest them. When images come under scrutiny, it is more often than not from conservative clergy condemning them on the basis of fundamentalist religious beliefs.

Like all citizens of this nation who passively endorse and perpetuate white supremacy with no obvious meaningful gain, black folks whose lives are shaped by the same values rarely discuss their motivation. Successful black and brown folks will at times emphasize that their willingness to assimilate into the dominant culture is the key to their making it in the world. Yet this assimilation comes with a price, for the dominant culture is also dominator culture. This means that in order to attain material success beyond the boundaries of economic necessity (that is, having the means to survive comfortably) they usually must collude in supporting the thinking and practice of white supremacy. As long as this collusion leads to greater material success it is an acceptable practice.

All citizens of this nation are encouraged to believe that material status will determine the degree of material well-being. As the economy fails and more folks than ever before in contemporary times lack material resources, magazines and newspaper articles assure them that the rich are happier, that money is the key to well-being. We are told that folks with material privilege are happier and healthier. No matter the daily news exposing widespread mental health problems and addiction among the wealthy, the fantasy that wealth equates with the good life, with optimal well-being, continues to be all-pervasive across class and race in the United States. It is evident that the vast majority of black people in our society do not live lives of optimal well-being. And it is equally evident that the persistence of white supremacist assault and everyday racism is a major culprit.

If we are to truly address issues of race and racism then our society must make the creation of the conditions for optimal well-being a central aspect of anti-racist struggle; however, this will require everyone to place psychological issues at the forefront. Issues of self-esteem will need to be primary; we will need to focus on defining and creating the necessary conditions wherein healthy self-esteem can be nurtured and can flourish. We will need to fully understand the process by which those folks with wounded and damaged self-esteem may be able to heal. In the best of all anti-racist scenarios, our society would create progressive mental care centers in local communities where issues of domination, of race and racism could be examined in a therapeutic context. In this case healthy self-esteem could serve as the foundation for a progressive anti-racist politics that could change how we all relate in everyday life.

We can hope that because the election of a black president has highlighted issues of race, our nation will be able to seize the opportunity to challenge white supremacy, going to the root of the matter and starting over from there. As more and more black folk enter the ranks of the poor and indigent, it is all the more crucial that they be given new ways of being and becoming. If this does not happen, widespread hopelessness and despair will be the norm. Without any hope of well-being, addiction becomes pervasive as folks seek to mediate and solace pain. Along with addiction then there is the violence, the rage that surfaces. Whether it is the racialized rage of poor white folks who see black people as the threat diminishing their quality of life or the internalized racialized rage that leads black folks to abuse one another psychologically and physically, this rage must be constructively addressed. As our nation talks race, there is at least the small hope that conversations can lead to new insights and strategies for change that will result in a world where all citizens can have access to optimal well-being.

3

Moving Past Blame: Embracing Diversity

Diversity is the reality of all our lives. It is the very essence of our planetary survival. Organically, human survival as a species relies on the interdependence of all life. Fundamentalist thinking, supporting dominator culture, denies this truth, socializing citizens to believe that safety resides in upholding the tyranny of the same, in protecting homogeneity. Describing what is meant by the dominator model in *The Power of Partnership: Seven Relationships That Will Change Your Life,* Riane Eisler writes: "Families and societies are based on control that is explicitly or implicitly backed up by guilt, fear, and force. The world is divided into in-groups and out-groups, with those who are different seen as enemies to be conquered or destroyed." When diversity first became a buzz word for the inclusion of difference in the academic world and the workplace, it was presented as a rather benign concept, another version of the myth of our nation as a genuine melting pot where differences meet and converge. This concept of diversity has held sway in most institutional settings—from grade schools, colleges and universities, to the corporate world.

Think for a moment about grade-schoolers learning that Columbus sailed the ocean blue, and was greeted by Indians who were only too happy to welcome white settlers. In this version of diversity, the center of imperialist white supremacist capitalist patriarchy as it has been constructed by the dominator culture remains unchanged; the addition of difference does not alter the construction of the center. Another example, and perhaps a more pertinent one for this discussion, is the election of the first black president of the United States. Many citizens view this change as a triumph for diversity. Yet as the presidency has unfolded, many of the decisions sanctioned by this black president seem no different than those of a liberal Christian white president. Indeed, much of the success of this presidency has been due to the fact that his dreaded difference has not really been that different. To many folks this represents a triumph for diversity. To those who know better it can only be seen as a veneer of difference making a change when the center stays the same. Today, the notion that diversity is vital to living in a global village where difference is truly the norm is commonly accepted. This acceptance is a sign of progress. Yet as many citizens, especially those who were and are truly different, soon learn (whether in schools or in the workplace), diversity is easy to talk about and hard to a make a lived reality. It is yet another case of theory without practice. Many people of color begin to see the evocation of diversity as a smokescreen obscuring the reality that those in mainstream power do not intend to change structures in even small ways so that there can be a genuine shift in thought and practice that will transform the worlds we inhabit day to day.

Diversity could not and cannot have meaningful transformative significance in any world where white supremacy remains the underlying foundation of thought and practice. A huge majority of unenlightened white folks believe that the mere presence of "difference" will change the tenor of institutions. And while no one can deny the positive power of diverse representation, representation alone is simply not enough to create a climate supportive of sustained diversity. Even though racial and ethnic integration brings a veneer of diversity, racism remains the norm. We talk about living in a diverse society, a global village, when the reality in the United States continues to be that most folks—even if they work in a diverse environment—choose to live and interact socially with people like themselves. Most neighborhoods in our nation continue to be segregated by race/ethnicity and class. While all around us folks in all spheres of public life talk about changing demographics (in particular the growing Hispanic population), few if any actions are taken to ensure that if, as James Baldwin proclaimed in "Stranger in the Village," "this world is white no longer, and it will never be white again," then the majority of people of color will not continue to be enslaved by the everyday practices of imperialist white supremacist capitalist patriarchy. Let us imagine that from the moment changing demographics became part of public awareness, public schools had created a curriculum that would require all students to learn Spanish, so that bilingual language skills would be acknowledged as a preferred norm. Then diversity would be affirmed. Without literacy, reading and writing, and ability to use computers, the changing demographics will not ensure that people of color of any group will have access to lives of optimal well-being. Without such skills masses of people of color, lacking the necessary resources both spiritual and material to create a sustainable life, will remain at the very bottom of our nation's economic totem pole.

Clearly the future of diversity lies in creating greater awareness and greater critical consciousness about the importance of ending domination, of challenging and changing white supremacy. Riane Eisler urges in her partnership model that we shift from an us-versus-them attitude to a worldview where we place the "same standards of human rights and responsibilities provided by the partnership model to all cultures." She contends: "In a world where technologies of communication and destruction span the globe almost instantaneously, creating a better world is a matter of enlightened self-interest." Now more than ever we need to create learning communities that make learning the theory and practice of diversity essential aspects of curriculum. In my recent book *Teaching Critical Thinking: Practical Wisdom,* I call attention to the way in which issues of diversity both inside and outside the classroom are slowly being pushed back into the realm of silence and misinformation. As I wrote: "More than ever before, students need to learn from unbiased perspectives, be they conservative or radical. More than ever before, students and teachers need to fully understand differences of nationality, race, sex, class, and sexuality if we are to create ways of knowing that reinforce education as the practice of freedom." Learning to challenge and change binary thinking—the us-and-them paradigm—is one way to create a foundation that can be sustained. Holding onto binary thinking actually keeps dominator culture in place, for one aspect of that culture is the projection outward onto an enemy, an "other," whenever things go wrong, and this casting of blame in turn helps to promote a culture of victimization.

When we are more energized by the practice of blaming than we are by efforts to create transformation, we not only cannot find relief from suffering, we are creating the conditions that help keep us stuck in the status quo. Our attachment to blaming, to identifying the oppressor stems from the fear that if we cannot unequivocally and absolutely state who the enemy is then we cannot know how to organize resistance struggle. In the insightful book *Ruling Your World: Ancient Strategies for Modern Life,* Mipham Rinpoche talks about learning to understand others rather than blaming them. He shares: "I remember my father and others of the older generation of Tibetan lamas saying that they did not blame the Communist Chinese for the destruction of Tibet. They felt that blaming the Chinese would not solve anything. It would only trap Tibetans in the past." Similarly, any critical examination of the history of the civil rights struggle in the United States will show that greater progress was made when leaders emphasized the importance of forgiving one's enemies, working for reconciliation and the formation of a beloved community, rather than angry retaliation.

Casting blame and calling for vengeance was an aspect of militant movements for black power that have really failed to sustain the climate of unlearning racism previously forged by nonviolent anti-racist struggle. In the aftermath of sixties rebellion, the more black folks were encouraged to vent rage, to "blame" all white folks for race-based exploitation and domination, and to eschew any notion of forgiveness, the more an internalized sense of victimhood became the norm. Tragically, today many black folks are more despairing of any possibility that racism can be effectively challenged and changed than at other similar historical moments when white supremacist aggression was more overtly life threatening. Unenlightened white folks who proclaim either that racism has ended or that they are not responsible for slavery engage a politics of blame wherein they disavow political reality to insist that black folk are never really victims of racism but are the agents of their own suffering.

Dualistic thinking, which is at the core of dominator thinking, teaches people that there is always the oppressed and the oppressor, a victim and a victimizer. Hence there is always someone to blame. Moving past the ideology of blame to a politics of accountability is a difficult move to make in a society where almost all political organizing, whether conservative or radical, has been structured around the binary of good guys and bad guys. Accountability is a much more complex issue. A politics of blame allows a contemporary white person to make statements like, "My family never owned slaves," or "Slavery is over. Why can't they just get over it?" In contrast, a politics of accountability would emphasize that all white people benefit from the privileges accrued from racist exploitation past and present and therefore are accountable for changing and transforming white supremacy and racism.

Accountability is a more expansive concept because it opens a field of possibility wherein we are all compelled to move beyond blame to see where our responsibility lies. Seeing clearly that we live within a dominator culture of imperialist white supremacist capitalist patriarchy, I am compelled to locate where my responsibility lies. In some circumstances I am more likely to be victimized by an aspect of that system, in other circumstances I am in a position to be a victimizer. If I only lay claim to those aspects of the system where I define myself as the oppressed and someone else as my oppressor, then I continually fail to see the larger picture. Any effort I might make to challenge domination is likely to fail if I am not looking accurately at the circumstances that create suffering, and thus seeing the larger picture. After more than thirty years of talking to folks about domination, I can testify that masses of folks in our society—both black and white—resist seeing the larger picture.

In working for justice, we must understand the roots of dominator thinking, because understanding the roots clarifies the actions we must take to resist. Reformist feminists continue to suggest that dominator culture begins with male subjugation of females. Yet this vision of how domination has become the norm is totally rooted in dualist thinking. It sets up males as the bad guys and females as the good guys. It has even led many white women to see racism as simply an extension of sexist thinking. Of course thinking this way allows for the perpetuation of a hierarchy of domination wherein sexism is deemed the more important system to challenge and change. In fact, recent evidence suggests that the first humans were probably all darker skinned people, which does not lend credence to the notion that sexism came first and then racism. Theories of domination that move us beyond blaming one group over another posit the notion that domination begins with the shift from a pre-agricultural society to one where agriculture has been domesticated. Interdependence was the norm in the world before agriculture. Carol Lee Flinders explains in *Rebalancing the World*: "Pre-agricultural human beings didn't see themselves as sharply separate from the natural world, or superior to it, but as members of one family or tribe among many others, doing their best to stay alive.... Before agriculture produced food surpluses, most all human beings were nomadic, gleaning from one locale and moving on in a few days to another within a defined territory. They traveled in bands, but the bands were small, reflecting the limited food resources of most places. Interdependence was the basic law of life: what you found or killed, you shared, knowing that if someone else got lucky the next day, he or she would reciprocate....Pre-agricultural people didn't imagine for a minute that they were masters of the world they surveyed....The keen sense of mutual reciprocity that defined one's relationship to the natural world defined one's relationship with the sacred as well." In this world, gender relations were more equitable as there were not clear demarcations between women's work and men's work. According to Flinders, it is the world of agriculture and settled territory that brought sharp gender divisions, artificially constructed paradigms of us and them, and war. It is not difficult to see how these early distinctions between us and them led to imperialist white supremacist capitalist patriarchy.

Strife over territory led to new behaviors by white people—a minority population whose color distinction and privilege is lost when breeding with those who are darker skinned to become more aggressive and warlike. The hoarding of material resources. The subjugation of women by men. The exploitation and oppression of the weak by the strong. In such a world system, dominator thinking and practice becomes the norm.

In *The Power of Partnership,* Eisler explains: "In the domination model, somebody has to be on top and somebody has to be on the bottom. Those on top control those below them. People learn, starting in early childhood, to obey orders without question. They learn to carry a harsh voice in their heads telling them they're no good, they don't deserve love, they need to be punished." Indoctrination into dominator thinking in a culture governed by the dictate of imperialist white supremacist capitalist patriarchy is a process that affects all of us to greater and lesser degrees. Understanding dominator thinking heightens the awareness that there is no simple way to identify victims and victimizers, although there are indeed degrees of accountability.

One of the most powerful counter-hegemonic narratives that can lead many of us down the path of critical consciousness is the idea of democracy. Certainly, prior to the sixties, it was learning about the global importance of democracy (i.e., that everyone had rights, that people were created equal, that there can be justice for all) that was the foundation of radicalization for many citizens of our nation. And this process of radicalization often began in early childhood. It often began with questioning why such an inspiring vision of democracy was not being fully realized. Today, as white children in my neighborhood learn about the Indians who resided here before white people, some, not all, begin to question: "Why did the white people have guns?" "Why did they kill the Indians or force them to leave their homes?" "Why did they take land that was already occupied?" In my childhood the right to ask "why" was a central privilege of living under the myth of democracy. And that myth was strong even though the more vital reality of our lives was the reality of patriarchal domination.

Even though origin stories which find the invention of patriarchy to be the root of domination may seem inaccurate, what is true is that in dominator culture the family is one of the primary pedagogical locations for the teaching of dominator thought and practice via the acceptance and perpetuation of patriarchy. Hence, working to challenge and change patriarchy continues to be essential to any effort to transform dominator culture. Progressive folks, especially prominent male thinkers and activists on the left, openly denounce imperialism, racism, and capitalism but rarely talk about the need to challenge patriarchy. And while all people of color, all black people, are socialized to embrace white supremacist thinking, few, if any, individuals from these constituents openly advocate racism. Individual black people who straighten their hair because they have been taught to believe their natural hair texture is ugly are perpetuating a white supremacist aesthetic even as they may be adamantly anti-racism. These contradictions reveal the myriad ways dominator culture shapes our thoughts and actions in ways that are unconscious. It is precisely because dominator thinking is so deeply embedded in our psyches that efforts to decolonize minds through the cultivation of critical consciousness needs to be an essential aspect of resistance struggle. When individuals who are psychologically confused engage in resistance struggle, they often are dysfunctional and act out in ways that undermine or negate their efforts to create constructive change. Since dominator culture relies on interlocking systems (imperialism, white supremacy, capitalism, patriarchy) to sustain itself, it seeks to cover up the connections between these systems. Or it allows for only one aspect of the system to be challenged at a time: for example, allowing anti-racist critiques while silencing anti-capitalist or anti-sexist voices.

And patriarchy begins at home. Again, it is the one aspect of dominator culture that we tend to learn from family, from folks who purport to care about us. In the past, patriarchal thinking learned in the family was mirrored in the patriarchal teachings of the church or other religious institutions. But, while religion was once a major forum for the teaching of racist thought, this is no longer an accepted norm. Christian white people are not overtly taught in church settings that god has ordained that they are superior to people of color and should rule over them. Indeed, even among the most fundamentalist Christians, there is a widespread effort to recruit people of color to join with them in worship. This welcoming stance is present even though churches in the United States are primarily racially segregated. Yet all the major religions of the world continue to openly teach patriarchal thinking. Concurrently, masses of people of color globally denounce white supremacy and racism while actively perpetuating patriarchy.

Nowadays many of our nation's citizens no longer attend church so the family has become the primary institution for the dissemination of patriarchal thought to children. Patriarchal females as primary caregivers of children are the people who teach patriarchal gender roles. Yet most males and females in our society rarely if ever use the word *patriarchy* or even understand its meaning. Patriarchy is a political and social system that insists males are inherently dominating, superior to everything and everyone deemed weak, especially females, and endowed with the right to dominate and rule over the weak as well as the right to maintain that dominance through various forms of psychological abuse and violence. No contemporary movement for social justice has changed the nature of how we live other than the feminist movement. Acknowledgment through law and public policy that women are the equals of men and deserve equal rights changed the nature of work, of economics, of home life. And while much is blamed on the feminist movement, the truth remains that females and males have greater access to gender equity in all spheres of life because of the feminist movement. It is precisely the myriad successes of feminist reform that have led to anti-feminist backlash.

Challenging and changing patriarchy threatens a core foundation of dominator culture. If boys are not socialized to embrace patriarchal masculinity and its concomitant violence, then they will not have the mindset needed to wage imperialist war. If females and males are taught to value mutuality, then partnership rather than the ethics of domination will be valued. Since patriarchal thinking creates psychological distress, new models of partnership offer the promise of well-being and therefore undermine the capitalist consumer culture, which exploits psychological pain. The positive changes created by the feminist movement were so widespread that the backlash has been fierce. Mass media, especially media targeting young children, teenagers, and young adults, continually reinscribes sexist thinking about gender roles. It has been the primary tool portraying feminists and/or powerful women in negative ways. In *The Power of Partnership*, Eisler emphasizes that one form anti-feminist backlash in media has taken is promoting "domination and submission in the relations between parents and children and between women and men." Explaining further she contends:

> The reason is that these intimate relations are where we first
> learn to accept domination and control as normal, inevitable,

and right....This is why many of the most repressive modern regimes...have sprung up where family and gender relations based on domination and submission are firmly in place. It is also why, once in power, these regimes have vigorously pushed policies that have as their goal the reinstatement of a punitive father in complete control of his family. We see this pattern all too clearly in one of the most serious aspects of the dominator regression of our time: the rise of so-called religious fundamentalism. I say *so-called* because, if we look closely, it's clear that what many fundamentalist leaders preach—be it in the Middle East or the United States—is not religious fundamentalism but the domination/control model with a religious spin.

Given the role patriarchy plays as a system that exploits familial relationships in order to teach dominator values, there are clear benefits to everyone—female and male, adult and child—when patriarchy is challenged and changed. Yet changing patriarchy will not bring an end to dominator culture as long as the other interlocking systems remain in place. When the feminist movement was bringing revolutionary changes to the status of women and men, imperialism, capitalism, and racism were all systems gaining strength globally.

When I first began to use the phrase *imperialist white supremacist capitalist patriarchy* to characterize the interlocking systems that shape the dominator culture we live within, individuals would often tell me that they thought it was just too harsh a phrase. In the past ten years, when I've used the phrase at lectures, more often than not audiences respond with laughter. Initially, I thought this laughter was an expression of discomfort, that the true nature of our nation's politics were being exposed. But as the laughter followed me from talk to talk I began to see it as a way to deflect attention away from the seriousness of this naming. Time and time again critical theory has taught us the power of naming accurately that which we are challenging and hoping to transform. But one way to silence accurate naming is to make it appear ridiculous, too strident, too harsh. Rarely am I asked the value of calling attention to interlocking systems of domination. Yet when we examine the cultural circumstances that provided the groundwork for fascism in the twentieth century (looking particularly at the roots of fascism in Germany, Spain, and Italy), we find similar traits in our nation (i.e., patriarchal, nationalistic, racist, religious, economic power controlled by a minority in the interests of wealth, religion, etc.). In fascist regimes, teaching populations to fear "terrorism" is one way the system garners support. Concurrently, dissident voices challenging the status quo tend to be silenced by varied forms of censorship. Most recently in our nation, the use of media to suggest that anyone who criticizes government is a traitor deserving of condemnation and even arrest effectively silences many voices.

Meaningful resistance to dominator culture demands of all of us a willingness to accurately identify the various systems that work together to promote injustice, exploitation, and oppression. To name interlocking systems of domination is one way to disrupt our wrong-minded reliance on dualistic thinking. Highlighted, these interlocking systems tend to indict us all in some way, making it impossible for any of us to claim that we are absolutely and always victims, calling attention to the reality of our accountability, however relative. When we are accountable, we eschew the role of victim and are able to claim the space of our individual and collective agency. For many folk, especially those who are suffering exploitation and/or oppression, that agency may seem inadequate. However, asserting agency, even in small ways, is always the first step in self-determination. It is the place of hope.

As we move away from dominator culture towards a liberatory culture where partnership and mutuality are valued we create a culture wherein we can all learn to love. There can be no love where there is domination. And anytime we do the work of love we are doing the work of ending domination. Engaging practices of active listening make bonding across differences viable. When we embrace diversity as a practice that can enrich, liberate, and transform our lives we are able to show by our actions that affirming diversity can revitalize ways of knowing, bring new energy to learning, and empower us to work for justice as we make education the practice of freedom. Fully embracing diversity is the way we can together work for change in ways that will help us all to live more fully, to live meaningful lives.

4

Solidarity: Women and Race Relations

When the issue of race is talked about in the United States it has always been seen as a contest between men. Yet when it comes to working with race, ultimately women do much of the hands-on work, as parents, as teachers, as cultural workers. Women teach generations of young minds what to think and know about race. And as a consequence of this gendered work, women of all races teach white supremacist thought and practice. Women teach what they know and what they have learned. Visionary thinkers on the issue of race all agree that were this nation able to confront the deep roots of race and racism we would all need to face white supremacist thought and practice; we would all need to look at the ways we are accountable for continually creating and maintaining this system of domination. To do this work necessitates seeing clearly the role women play in supporting and perpetuating racism.

Given the powerful role women have played throughout the history of this nation in both the perpetuation of white supremacy and the resistance struggle against racism, it is essential that we look at women if we are to truly understand how this drama plays itself out in our world today. The contemporary feminist movement pushed the discourse of race and racism in the United States in far more progressive directions than any other liberation struggle. Significantly, radical visionary feminist insistence that we examine the intersections of race, sex, and class has forged a new foundation for understanding race. It began to create a context for feminist solidarity between masses of women across race and class. It started a profound focus on whiteness, white privilege. And it allowed women to see clearly that a politically grounded solidarity across race was utterly threatening to imperialist white supremacist capitalist patriarchy. As feminist thinking and practice has gained power and momentum, creating a revolution of values in our lives, so has the anti-feminist backlash.

Looking critically at the role women are playing in discussions of race and racism it is easy to see how patriarchal thinking, especially as it is transmitted through mass media, has exploited notions of sisterhood and female solidarity so as to stoke the fires that aim to burn away all evidence of feminist consciousness raising, all evidence that women can bond across race to establish forms of solidarity that enable us all to have greater access to lives of optimal well-being. Given the patriarchal white supremacist anti-feminist backlash, it is crucial that we turn our attention once again to the ways women relate along the issues of race, that we look at the ways individual unenlightened white women are linking struggles for female advancement with the maintenance of white supremacy.

Critical thinking about the historical relationship between white women and black women reveals the extent to which these two groups are pitted against one another by dominator culture in ways that serve to maintain the status quo. Basically the message these two groups have historically received from dominator culture is that one group cannot be liberated unless the other group remains enslaved. It is the understanding of this message that has made and continues to make most black women fearful of alliances with white women, fearful that any gains white women make in the existing social structure will mean setbacks for black women/women of color. Retrospectively, it is evident that as long as women have sought solely to gain power within the existing social structure this has been the correct assumption.

The feminist movement may have placed the call for sisterhood on the political agenda, but the vast majority of white women were not prepared in their psyches to fully investigate and understand the class differences coupled with race that would and did make bonding between the two groups difficult, if not all but impossible. Historically the relationship between white women and black women had been characterized by domination, by white females exerting power over black females. And it was in the domestic household that this unequal relationship was most apparent. Two comments made by grown black women about their work in the domestic world of white folks stayed with me when I was growing up in the segregated world of the south. Mama was in pure organic critical consciousness mode when she told me repeatedly, "you can take what white folks have to offer, but you don't have to love them." The second comment was frequently made by black women working as domestics, who would declare with great vigor: "I've never seen a white woman over the age of twelve that I can respect." Mama worked now and then as a domestic in the homes of white women as did other black women in our community. They rarely shared any liking for the white women they worked for. Most importantly they shared disgust for the nasty shape the homes they worked in were kept and for what they took to be the overall laziness of white female employers.

White women may have been accorded higher status based on race but black females saw themselves as the true and better homemakers. Mama was approaching midlife when she first began to do occasional work as a domestic in white households. What most astonished her, this black female who had lived all her life in the segregated world of black culture, who had largely lived all her life supported financially by a husband who did not want his wife to work outside the home, who had grown up in a world that had always held white women in higher esteem, was the disorder and general uncleanness of white households. She could not believe the way white folks threw their dirty clothes on the floor and just left them there, underwear and all. When deconstructed, this level of "filth"—the word black women used to describe what they saw in white households—projected racialized fantasies about the pure and better nature of white female identity. Very few black women, Mama included, had seen any filth in the modest homes of working-class black folks. In early feminist writings I described these black domestics as organic anthropologists who would bring home from their journeys into whiteness their observations and their critiques. Not once did I hear any black females working as domestics in white households talk about their love for the white families they knew intimately. In my girlhood, listening to grown black women talk about working for white women, what I heard was the mistrust, the resentment, the overall contempt these black women felt toward white women employers.

When I began teaching a course focusing on African American Women Writers at Yale University, my classes were often stages for great conflict and drama between white and black females who clearly saw the world from completely different perspectives. I have vivid memories of a class where a white female student was sharing how much the black domestic caregiver in her home "loved" the family and how much they loved her. When I asked her to share how she knew that the black woman caretaker loved her "white folks," she had no answers. Yet she became terribly emotionally distraught when it was suggested to her that the black woman who cared for them might have pretended to feel affection while really repressing ongoing rage and resentment toward all white people, including those she worked for. At this point the student became enraged at the class for daring to interrogate her sentimental construction of the relationship between black women domestics and the white families they care for. Then and in more recent times, I am reminded of how important it appears to be for white folks, especially those living within white supremacist dominator culture, to believe they are loved by their black female employees. This notion that folks in positions of powerlessness are somehow able to transcend exploitation, oppression, or simply unjust circumstances and offer love to those who exert power over them—is a fantasy.

Certainly I and other students in the class whose mothers had worked in the homes of white folks had never heard them speak of loving their white charges. While we had heard them speak of affection for white children, mostly they expressed resentment about the hard work and low wages paid to them by white adults, as well as the dehumanizing interactions they experienced while on the job. In her insightful book *Between Women: Domestics and Their Employers,* sociologist Judith Rollins examines both the perspectives of black women working as domestics and the white women who hired them. Documenting no talk of bonding with love from either group, she shares the complexity of dominator culture as it impacts women working for women in the domestic household. Rollins's work reveals that there was a clear recognition of the way in which race and class differences have militated against the formation of bonds of affection.

One white woman employer openly shared her struggle with the ethical issue of hiring domestic servants at a time when the women's liberation movement was calling attention to the devaluation of domestic labor. She was affected by "the ethical questions" that were involved when the women's movement called attention to "the exploitation involved in one woman feeling that she should be free from the shit-work at home and requiring somebody else to do that." Explaining further, she stated: "I realize I have had a problem hiring help because of my guilt and my concern about exploiting people....Can you have a business-like deal in a house?...Who would put up with that shit by choice? Why would you choose something that's low-paid, that doesn't give you protection and that doesn't give you status?

And there's so little pleasure in it!" Although often talked about by black women, this type of honest reflection on the race, class, and gender cultural backdrop women faced and face when dealing with the issue of relationships between women in the arena of domestic work has rarely been openly discussed by white women.

On those rare occasions when white women have been questioned about their relationships with the black women domestics, many white women employers like to suggest that bonds of affection and shared sisterhood existed and exist between the two groups. The white female need to humanize a relationship that was and is more often than not dehumanizing is consistently evident when white and black women interact. And since the power and status that whiteness offers to white women—the "privilege" of being the one who defines reality—it makes perfect sense that many white females hiring black women for low wages, exploiting both their time and their image, need to believe that positive connections outweigh any negative interactions.

Individual black women/women of color were among the first group of enlightened feminist thinkers to interrogate intersections of race and gender, whereby white women and black women are pitted against one another in such a way as to show the flaws and faults of the other group. Since devaluation of black womanhood from slavery to the present day has led to the consistent representation of black females as powerful, aggressive, angry, and ultimately irrational to the point of outright insanity, this has been the perfect foil for those white women who show continued allegiance to patriarchy and who are then represented as powerless, submissive, and willing to take orders and subordinate themselves to the will of the more "rational," dominant men. Significantly, these neat binary racialized sexist stereotypes were disrupted when the feminist movement not only shifted the nature of gender roles but revealed the very real extent to which some white women were eager to assert power, to show aggression, and to act like the patriarchal men the women's liberation movement critiqued. As white female power in all its forms came out of the closet, it seemed a matter of course that the mass media began to construct images of black and white females fighting each other for the position of dominant female. Whereas the category "bitch" had been used against black women to dehumanize us and condone exploitation and oppression, white women began to call themselves "bitches" as a label of power and pride.

When Hillary Clinton entered the White House her presence was initially perceived to be a victory for women's liberation. She was not standing behind her man; she gave the world the image of the new independent woman standing beside her man in equal partnership. Her use of power was swiftly mocked in patriarchal media. Like the negative representations that have plagued all black women, she was depicted as emasculating and castrating, depicted as an engulfing mad vagina eager to devour the patriarchal male. Clinton, viewed worldwide as a feminist icon, was perceived to embody a dangerous threat: the possibility of feminism overtaking this country, if not the world. When the presidential election pitted Clinton against Obama, race and gender once again were pitted against one another. To stand for Hillary was to stand with feminism. To stand with Barack was to stand with a revitalizing patriarchy.

When feminist thinking and practice first became the norm for many white females, black women were endeavoring to understand whether it would be in our collective best interest to support feminist movement. Most black women saw women's liberation both in its inception and in its present form as only serving to bring white women more power and thereby giving white women more power to rule over black females and all black people. And even though visionary feminist thinkers offered a more insightful understanding of the interconnections of race, class, and gender, the mass public did not read our work. Despite our call for a sisterhood based on a realistic understanding of differences and a call for solidarity between women, black females mostly continued to feel that they could not trust white females to protect their interests and that given a chance most white females would seek to dominate black females.

Racialized sexism has pitted black females against white females from slavery on into the present day, and black females have more often than not been the losers in this contest to see who embodies the more perfect vision of acceptable womanhood. That status quo was challenged in 1959 when Douglas Sirk's melodramatic film *Imitation of Life* became a box office success. Offering an insightful critique in *Where the Girls Are: Growing Up Female with the Mass Media*, Susan Douglas shows the way in which dominant mass media culture pitted black and white females against one another:

> What's especially interesting here is the reversal Sirk does: the fair, blond woman is self-centered and bad, the darker woman is Christ-like and good. Usually in popular culture it was the other way around, although black women, when they got movie or TV roles at all, could only be selfless earth mothers who spoke in malapropisms and loved white children more than their own. We see here how black women and white women were used against each other in American popular culture, the white woman embodying standards of beauty impossible for black women to achieve, but the black woman serving as a powerful moral rebuke to the self-indulgent narcissism of the white woman who dares to think for herself.

These dynamics might easily describe the contemporary competition between Hillary Clinton's image and that of Michelle Obama, where once again the question was posed "will the real woman please stand up."

Tragically, this racialized sexism and the melodramatic war between black and white females that it evokes remains a norm in white supremacist culture. And nowhere has that been more evident than during the presidential campaign of Barack Obama. More often than not conservative right-wing media represented Michelle Obama as a violent, castrating, aggressive, controlling black woman. Following in the wake of Hillary Clinton, whose perceived feminist leanings had alienated a huge majority of the American public who regarded her as too controlling, as castrating and in the very worst-case scenario, man-hating, Michelle Obama was initially depicted as potentially even worse than Hillary Clinton. To counter that image both in the campaign and in their successful election to the White House the Obamas proclaimed to the world that family life in the White House would definitely be organized along traditional, all be it benevolent, patriarchal lines. Suddenly, Michelle Obama's image was constructed as the polar opposite of Hillary Clinton's. Like the Douglas Sirk image of the selfless earth mother, Michelle Obama was represented as primarily concerned about her family. After the election she was increasingly represented as the embodiment of the perfect wife and mother standing just enough behind her man to let the world know that he was in control.

During her 2008 DNC convention speech, Michelle Obama declared: "I come here as a wife who loves my husband and believes he will be an extraordinary president. I come here as a mom, as a mom whose girls are the heart of my heart and the center of my world—they're the first things I think about when I wake up in the morning, and the last thing I think about before I go to bed at night. Their future—and all our children's future—is my stake in this election." From that moment on, Michelle Obama consistently reassured the nation that she would not be like Hillary Clinton, that her contribution would be to focus on family, both her family and the nation's families.

Headlines in women's magazines celebrated the triumph of sacrificial motherhood in the White House. Indeed, Michelle Obama began to talk of herself as "mom in chief." Whether unwittingly or not, Michelle Obama's representation was used to undermine the feminist movement, to make it appear that even though a woman might be a Harvard-educated lawyer, so brilliant her professors believed she would make an excellent presidential candidate herself, her primary and most important role in life was that of wife and mother. And when he was asked about her role in the White House, her husband let the world know that she would not be helping to run the government, she would be taking care of family matters. The age-old use of black females to remind white females and all females that subservience remains the ideal position for a female in the sexist order is still in place. Its insistence that the most subordinated woman will be "queen for the day" continues to operate as the force pitting groups of women against one another.

Whether it is the entertaining novels of white South African writer Alexander McCall Smith who uses the body of a traditionally built (i.e., fat) black female; the character of Precious to speak the differences between negative "liberated" white females and their more accepting black female counterparts; or movies that show black females being chosen over the feisty white female who is out of line, the most positive representation of a black female is still that of the long-suffering matriarch. That image competes with the representation of black females as dangerous bitches. In Chris Rock's comedy special *Kill the Messenger,* he tells the world that we cannot have a black female in the White House because she will try to rule, because she will refuse subordination. Overall, it is clearly evident that despite women's liberation, in the world of white supremacist capitalist patriarchy, women must compete to be chosen as the embodiment of perfect womanhood and that such competition must be encouraged to continue so as to prevent bonds of solidarity between women across class and race.

In the early stages of the feminist movement women worked to name and resist these negative stereotypes. Calling for an understanding of differences, of the way in which whiteness accords white privilege to white women, including the right to lord it over black women/women of color, feminist theory asked that all women develop critical consciousness and the skills to critically examine and defy patriarchy. The intent was to both acknowledge the reality of difference in positionality and perspective while at the same time calling for females to use that understanding and awareness to serve as the basis for construction of a platform of political solidarity that would serve the interests of all women and men committed to challenging and changing patriarchy. Concurrently, women were encouraged to recognize shared experience and common bonds of sisterhood, while simultaneously refusing any sentimental construction of female bonding that would prevent us from recognizing class and race hierarchies and the difference those hierarchies create.

Within small circles of the visionary feminist movement, the aims of sisterhood were often realized. Within mainstream culture, however, sentimental notions of sisterhood not only became the norm, they were celebrated. Women bonding was no longer leading to political solidarity in the interest of challenging and changing patriarchy, it was all reduced to personal intimacy. Books like *The Color Purple, Paradise, Divine Secrets of the Ya-Ya Sisterhood, The Secret Life of Bees,* and so on offered images of a world of everyday female bonding that had no connection to organized feminist political struggle. Many of the movies and books that purported to show a world of celebratory woman bonding simply reinforced the thinking and practices of imperialist white supremacist capitalist patriarchy.

Movies like *It's Complicated* wherein the middle-aged white woman played by actress Meryl Streep is the long-suffering Jane, who is in long-term recovery from the breakup of her marriage to Jake (played by Alec Baldwin), epitomize this sentimental portrait. The betraying, unfaithful Jake left Jane ten years earlier for a younger wife who is darker-skinned, beautiful, self-centered, and potentially dominating. Represented as sensual and exotic, she is the mother of a darker-skinned boy, Pedro, who is depicted as Mr. Macho, ruling both his mother and stepfather. When Jane and Jake begin a sexual affair, she sits in a circle of her girlfriends, all white women like herself, and crows with triumph: she is besting the younger woman through her betrayal. It is the perfect revenge. No mention is ever made of the younger woman's ethnicity, but it is clear that she does not share in the privileged "whiteness" that connects Jane and her circles of sisterhood.

The message of the movie suggests that it is acceptable for white women to show allegiance and fierce loyalty to women like themselves while destroying the lives of women unlike themselves. So much for feminist solidarity. It is hard to decide which is more dangerous, the proliferation of books and movies that pit white and black females against one another or the many recent books and movies which portray black females in the "mammy" position providing the white women's lovely white grown-up children with strategies for survival.

The recent successful publication of Kathryn Stockett's book *The Help* is a perfect example of this trend. Writing from the standpoint of black domestics in the 1960s, Stockett has her black characters reveal, as Stockett tells it, "truths" about themselves and the white women for whom they work. In an afterword at the end of the book, Stockett acknowledges that she was raised for a time by a black domestic. Boldly, she announces: "I was afraid I would fail to describe a relationship that was so intensely influential in my life, so loving, yet so grossly stereotypical in American history and literature." Evidently she overcame this fear, because her book is as grossly stereotypical as any fictional book in the history of American letters, which purports to give us the inside look into relationships between black domestics and the white women they serve.

Continuing her self-praise in the afterword, Stockett tells readers that there is one sentence in the book she prizes above all others. Her white female "writer" protagonist declares about her relationship to a black female: "Wasn't that the point of the book? For women to realize, we are just two people. Not that much separates us. Not nearly as much as I'd thought." Needless to say there is nothing that suggests that the writer of this amazingly successful first novel has learned anything from feminist theory or from cultural critics who study the dynamics of race and representation. She need not interrogate her position, her values, her politics before she begins writing.

Of course, as Richard Dyer highlights in his discussion of white privilege in the cultural treatise *White,* the reality is simply that white folks are not called on to question the assumptions they make about the lives and voices of non-white others. Dyer explains:

> As long as whiteness is felt to be the human condition, then it alone both defines normality and fully inhabits it...the equation of being white with being human secures a position of power. White people have power and believe that they think, feel and act like and for all people; white people, unable to see their particularity, cannot take account of other people's; white people create the dominant images of the world and don't quite see that they thus construct the world in their own image; white people set standards of humanity by which they are bound to succeed and others bound to fail.

This passage is worth quoting at length because it illuminates the overall narcissism underlying the creation of Stockett's black characters, who speak in a dialect more suited to historical periods of extreme Jim Crow racial segregation than modern times. Many of the lines she uses appear to be directly mimicking lines from Walker's *The Color Purple,* which was certainly full of stereotypical images even as Walker juxtaposed these old images with radical representation.

One might indeed see Stockett's work as following in a long line of sentimental darky stories that aim to tell the world that positive emotional connections forged between oppressor and oppressed, exploiter and exploited, are more powerful than dehumanizing practices. While history documents the extent to which individuals on all sides can at times, in circumstances of domination, prevail against hate and create positive bonds, this experience has never been and is not common. Indeed, Stockett does not examine her failure to maintain connection with the black domestic she now claims to have "loved" so much. Certainly it has been easier for black females, enslaved and free, to develop ties of affection toward innocent white children than to the many grown white folks who sanctioned everyday racism and its various cruel, abusive, and unkind acts. In the revealing autobiography of her wealthy Kentucky plantation family, Sally Bingham documents the way in which her family would denigrate "niggers" at the dinner table as though the black folks who were serving them were invisible, or deaf. These social enactments of white supremacist privilege do not leave the scars left behind by harsh physical punishment or brutal verbal abuse, but no matter the response of an individual black person—however patient, accepting, or kind to white owners or employers—soul murder was more often than not taking place. And the black person so dominated was diminished.

No doubt this is one of the reasons black folk, especially black women working as domestics, often talked more in the privacy of their homes about the unkindness and cruelty of white women rather than about ties of affection. I can remember one name of a white woman for whom mama was a domestic. I can remember this woman's name because mama talked about her as a kind and just employer. I do not remember any of the grown people I grew up with in the segregated world of our town talking about loving, or even liking, white folks. Admiration sometimes, envy, jealousy, awe, even, but never declarations of love. This was equally true of the circle of black women who were mama's colleagues and friends. Yet Stockett's has no hesitation in proclaiming: "There was so much more love between white families and black domestics than I had the ink or the time to portray." Given white supremacist thinking, should it surprise anyone that we primarily hear of this mythical love from white women?

Kathryn Stockett acknowledges in her afterword that as a girl she looked upon black people with disdain and pity, declaring, "I am so embarrassed to admit that now" and confessing that she believed that

Demetrie, the black woman who cared for her and her siblings, was "lucky to have us." Nowhere, either in her fictional account or in her autobiographical justifications at the end of this first novel, does she share whether or not she has created her black domestic characters from an anti-racist pro-feminist perspective. It is difficult to imagine the actual relationships that inspired this book since the "beloved" black female caregiver she praises was soon forgotten when Stockett entered her teens. Yet as she remembers her, she is able to extend "belated thanks to Demetrie McLorn, who carried us all out of the hospital wrapped in our baby blankets and spent her life feeding us, picking up after us, loving us, and, thank God, forgiving us." Note that as Richard Dyer highlights in *White,* Stockett as a white authority figure need not document in any way how it was that she understood the emotional feelings of her adult black woman caregiver, especially how the modern-day mammy figure she has constructed from childhood memory extended her forgiveness.

For those individual black women/women of color and our white women allies in struggle who have spent years working to unpack buried and forgotten history, who have worked to take all women's lives out of the realm of white supremacist patriarchal projection and fantasy so that everyone might have clear and accurate understanding of the real lives of real women, fictions like Stockett's act as obstructions. We have all had folks tell us about this book, describing it as a documentary history. And yet even when they are told that this is a work of problematic fiction, some white women choose to use it in their classrooms, ignoring insightful critiques. After all, why should they have to heed the insights of learned women of color and white women when they, like Stockett, use white privilege to assert that they know more and better than us mere scholars, critical thinkers, and book writers.

Significantly, one of the most crucial interventions visionary feminist thinkers made was to acknowledge that one way we all might divest of race, class, and gender privilege is by letting whomever it is we deem "other" speak in their own voice. We urged women, especially the downtrodden, the forgotten, the disenfranchised to search within and find the words to tell their own stories. This did not carry any absolute insistence that we not speak at times on behalf of others, or that we never use our voices of privilege to tell the story of women whom circumstance has rendered them powerless, but rather that we bring mindful awareness of the dangers that arise when appropriating the stories that we know only through hearsay or limited imagination and raising them to the level of gospel truth. There are individual black female writers who have created female characters as flawed and cartoonish as the characters in *The Help*. They, like Stockett, are accountable for the images they produce, especially when they sell their work in a mainstream marketplace that on all fronts is dominated and controlled by folks who have rarely made a commitment to unlearning racism or ending white supremacy. Stockett's work is not the lone contribution of one white woman. No doubt there is a circle of educated white folks who have made this book a monetary success, from the first folks who read it to the many white reviewers who tell us how wonderful it is.

Every aware white woman, black woman/woman of color writing and selling books knows that decolonized images of black females do not sell as well as images that colonize, that reproduce racist and sexist stereotypes. For a brief moment during the peak of the contemporary feminist movement in our nation's history, the voices of black/ women of color writers gained a powerful hearing. And a variety of voices and perspectives emerged; some of those voices were conservative, others reinforced the existing status quo, a few were radical. Then, as the world of publishing and marketing changed, it was not works by feminist black women and women of color that grew in shape and quantity. Instead, we became the subjects of writing by a new breed of young, educated white women who see themselves as the best spokespersons to tell the world about the reality of how women of color truly are and how they live their lives. A perfect example of this trend is the journalistic creative nonfiction *The Immortal Life of Henrietta Lacks* by white writer Rebecca Skloot.

Ironically, although Michelle Obama—one of the most visible black females in our nation—is a woman who has been educated at Harvard and has worked at the height of her legal profession, she has basically been silenced by public demand that she not act like a "feminist" (i.e., that she not act like Hillary Clinton). We are bombarded with white women providing us with their version of black woman minstrel speak, while real black women are forced into silence. Feminist poet Audre Lorde has already shared the insight that "when we speak we are afraid our words will not be heard nor welcomed," yet she tells us "but when we are silent we are still afraid, so it is better to speak." In their own way the sentimental books that focus on cozy female bonding that just happens to cross race, class, and sexuality (because women all share a common reality) undercut the feminist work that teaches everyone to look not just at what brings females together superficially across differences now and then, but rather at what keeps us apart more often than not. Feminist thinkers demand that we examine those forces that separate us and pit us against one another while holding us hostage to patriarchal thinking and values. Within patriarchy women are encouraged to constantly compete against one another, to see one another as enemies. The pseudo-sisterhood sentimental novel and the world of funky fun sisterhood it projects does not change this reality.

That such work abounds would not seem like such a dangerous trend if these *Imitation of Life* fictions (like Stockett's, which has been turned into a Hollywood film) were published alongside many other works springing from the decolonized imaginations of enlightened women and men of all races, and especially women of color. Are readers surprised that privileged white women who are among the major book buyers in our nation would rather read melodramatic fictions that provide sentimental fantasies of relationships between black and white women rather than hear stories, whether fictitious or fully documented, that would speak more fully about rage, anger, and hatred, as well as bonds of affection. No doubt it will take a profoundly honest writer to tell true stories, no matter how few in number, of how the colonizer and the colonized can come together in resistance and learn to care deeply for one another, to care in ways that are reciprocal and mutual.

Writing, whether fiction or nonfiction, which centers on the lives of women while pushing narratives that are essentially anti-feminist, narratives which are often most marketed by patriarchal male marketing and reviewing, both instigate and collude with anti-feminist backlash. A fine example of this might also be Elizabeth Gilbert's bestselling memoir *Eat, Pray, Love,* which mostly uses a crew of exotic people of color as the colorful supportive backdrop to a white woman's journey toward self-actualization. As her memoir draws to a close, Gilbert tells readers that she has "no nostalgia for the patriarchy, please believe me. But what I have come to realize is that when that patriarchic system was (rightfully) dismantled it was not necessarily replaced by another form of protection." Comments like this help add to the popular fantasy that patriarchy has ended and that there really is no need for the feminist movement. In their brilliant critique of Gilbert's book in *Bitch* magazine, Joshunda Sanders and Diana Barnes-Brown explain this trend: "It's no secret that, according to America's marketing machine, we're living in a 'postfeminist' world where what many people mean by 'empowerment' is the power to spend their own money....Such marketing, and the women who buy into it, assumes the work of feminism is largely done....This perspective makes it easy for the antifeminism embedded in the wellness jargon of priv-lit to gain momentum." Because this anti-feminist thinking is often hidden, it is an easy sell.

In Kathryn Stockett's novel, readers are told that "the help always knows." Even so, the dominant culture has shown little interest in hearing the voices of the help, especially when the voices are poor, black, and female. Clearly, the popularity of Stockett's book, as well as the many bestselling sentimental novels preceding her work written by women of all races, is positive only to the extent that it suggests white, black, and women of all other colors are eager to understand one another. Genuine understanding must be rooted in a rejection of dominator culture. And as women and men committed to challenging and changing dominator culture and eliminating racism, patriarchy, and class elitism, we can only hope that this longing to know the other will lead folks to yearn to hear one another speak in honest mutual dialogue. That dialogue can only take place when a spirit of resistance prevails, one that emerges when women dare to speak truth together and on that basis create the foundation for a true and lasting feminist-based sisterhood.

When women choose to unite to challenge white supremacy, a profound revolution of values will take place. Love of justice will be expressed by changing thought and action. Visionary feminist thinkers have already shown everyone that we can choose to be disloyal to dominator culture, that we can indeed create bonds of solidarity that help us heal from all the traumatic wounds caused by racial assault as well as the traumas of sexist and classist oppression.

When the world truly listens to the voices of women who have and are daily working to decolonize our minds, who live in the joy of that transformation, we can all walk the path to greater liberation, to solidarity. This shared journey will bring us to a place of peace and possibility. Then we will not need to shore up wounded spirits by creating false sentiment fictions to hide in; and we can embrace the truths that do indeed set us free.

5

Help Wanted: Re-Imagining The Past

Writing about the successful publication of Kathryn Stockett's novel *The Help* in an essay that looks at the way women create public narratives about race, I emphasize that it is precisely the book's failure to offer any meaningful fictionalized accounts of the relationships between white women and black female domestics in the 1960s which, ironically, is one of the reasons it has been such a success. The book and the movie tell audiences very little about race and racism in the deep south; however, they do tell story after story about the way women, and particularly white women, interact with one another and with the black females who work for them. Stockett's fictional work was and is a supreme triumph of bad writing. Like the early sentimental novels her work resembles, she distorts, exaggerates, and generally misrepresents the lives of southern white women and black female domestics in order to create a world of female cruelty where sisterhood and solidarity triumph in the end. Instead of the Victorian trope "reader, I married him," the happily-ever-after closing audiences get in these books is "reader, I am free." Profound message of the moment: "telling your story makes you free."

Despite its many flaws, the extreme melodramatic fictionalization of the 1960s plight of black female domestics who, confronting legal racial segregation and terrible inequalities, had no choice but to serve in white homes, the novel *The Help* does attempt moments of seriousness. However, the film turns the entire story into farce and places actual civil rights struggle so far in the background that it barely merits ten minutes of screen time. This re-positioning affords moviemakers the space to ignore historical accuracy and offer a version of civil rights struggle that is entirely taking place between vicious unenlightened white women and exploited black female domestics. Both the book and the film adaptation attempt to evoke nostalgia for the old south, when white supremacy and class hierarchy ruled social mores, while at the same time occasionally attempting to call attention to flaws in that system.

Seen within the political culture and social backdrop of our time, wherein the greatest symbolic challenge to imperialist white supremacist capitalist patriarchy has occurred (the placement of a biracial black male in the White House and his black wife and children) the publication of *The Help* can only be seen as backlash, both against the movement to end racism and the feminist movement. There simply is no way that the book *The Help,* mediocre sentimental fiction that it is, has become a bestseller on merit. Indeed, had the book not been supported and fully backed by a conservative white-male-dominated publishing and advertising empire no one would have ever heard of this work and certainly very few readers would have pored over its pages. No doubt, from the moment it was purchased this manu-script was positioned by editors and marketing forces to be sensational and to cause a sensation. How could it not be outrageous that at a historical moment when Michelle Obama, the most famous black female in the world, is living in the White House and being served by domestics, many of them white, that the most popular book and movie consumed around the world seeks to hold up the exploited, abused black female domestic worker in the south as the true embodiment of desirable womanhood.

Of course this narrative parallels Michele Obama's own self-caricature as "mom in chief." In order to separate herself from the image of feminist ball breaker associated with Hillary Clinton, Michelle Obama chose to represent herself first and foremost as always and only obsessed with caring for her family. Many people forget that Clinton had dubbed herself the "family feminist"—a term that powerful white woman Laura Ingraham in her hateful polemic *The Hillary Trap: Looking for Power in All the Wrong Places* argued represented "the False Sisterhood Trap." In her polemical work Ingraham was so eager to trash Hillary Clinton that she never engaged in the self-critiques that would have helped her to see that she had mad aggression whenever Clinton was mentioned.

Ingraham's work reeks of disrespect, and that tone has nothing to do with the right or wrongness of her critical insights. Note the paradox. On one hand she explains: "Hillary is such an unlikely role model for a self-respecting woman, if you think about it. I don't care how many inspirational speeches she gives while she's globe-trotting at taxpayer's expense about bringing 'new dignity and respect to women and girls all over the world.' A prominent woman in the public eye who puts up with chronic marital infidelities…is not standing up for women's dignity. It's even worse when she colludes in trashing women victimized by her husband's egregious sexual misconduct and attempts to excuse his behavior by blaming his dead mother and grandmother." Despite the vicious tone underlying these comments, a few lines down Ingraham contends: "The only kind of sisterhood that can work is one in which we treat each other with decency and respect as people, even as we respectfully disagree about issues." There is no respect offered Clinton in this work.

Can the American public be surprised then that Michelle Obama and the handlers shaping her representation felt such a deep need to divorce her politics from those of Hillary Clinton, especially her feminist politics? By cutting herself off from feminist politics, Michelle Obama has succeeded in shaping a new image for a White House wife, and this choice has had far-reaching negative consequences for females and males of all races who are anti-sexist and who proudly advocate feminism, not to mention the negative impact on masses of citizens who doubt the movement's value. Throughout her tenure in the White House Obama has singlehandedly bolstered anti-feminist backlash by making it appear that a woman in the White House as wife and mother could not also be progressive and politically powerful in every other way.

To the extent that Michelle Obama, along with the individuals who helped shape her public image, highlighted her dedication to family, she has created a narrative that to some extent is totally in sync with the narrative of *The Help,* both book and movie. There are many stories told in *The Help,* but the primary one is that black female domestics were the surrogate mothers and caregivers in white families. The old saying "we love white folks more than they love themselves" certainly holds true in the fictive culture of whiteness created in *The Help.* Despite the incredible marketing success of the book, it is the film that most carries this message of black female loyalty and devotion to their white charges, whether they are "mammy" to small white children or mammies wiping the asses and tears of grown white women. When the protagonist Skeeter (the white woman who decides to make a splash as a writer by interviewing black maids) publishes her book, it is the black preacher who gives Aibileen, the maid assisting Skeeter, the copy to present to her that everyone has signed declaring, "this is for the white lady. You tell her we love her, like she's our own family."

In the film almost all the black female domestics are depicted as dark skinned with distorted features and overweight bodies. When viewers are shown a scene of Aibileen soaking in the tub, her body drenched in sweat, her flesh looks as though it has been burnt, a representation eerily reminiscent of images of lynched and burnt black bodies. And of course Aibileen's crime is that she cares for and loves the white children she tends. Even though she is portrayed as traumatized by the death of her beloved son almost to the point of dehumanization, she is able to be re-humanized via her loving engagement with white children. It is she who rescues the discarded emotionally abandoned baby girl Mae and offers her affirmations aimed at laying a foundation for healthy self-esteem. In a child-like, silly sounding white version of black dialect she tells Mae "you is smart, you is kind, you is important." It is Mae Mobley who insists on declaring: "Ibee, you're my real mama." She goes on to happily declare, "I's your baby....I'm your real baby." Viewers of course never know whether these loving affirmations will have any long range positive impacts on Mae, since we last see her screaming and crying for Aibileen, who has been forced to abandon her. No doubt without any meaningful emotional object constancy, Mae will likely adopt the mean-spirited habits of the adult white women who surround her.

The representation of Mae is in direct contrast to that of Skeeter, the filmic white heroine who is daring to go behind the scenes to tell the stories that will "liberate" her and help her black female informants have better lives. Skeeter has had emotional object constancy. Raised by an elder black female, Constantine, she has been nurtured and tenderly cared for. It is Skeeter who confronts her mother and calls out not only the white females' emotional abandonment of their children but also their willful disregard of the surrogate black mothers who assume the role of caregivers. Ironically the one black female in an intact hetero-normative family who, with her husband, consistently cares for her two boys, is depicted as a thief forced by circumstance to steal for her children's well-being. While her cruel white woman employer sits in a car next to her blond white male child, Yula Mae is arrested and beaten, thereby being forced to abandon her boys.

A recurring question Skeeter, in her role as investigative journalist, asks Aibileen centers around the issue of how she must have felt to leave her own children "motherless" while "mothering" white children. Although this question is raised several times, it is never answered. The silence surrounding this question implies the existence of a story so painful and traumatic it cannot be spoken. Black females cannot talk about the impact of their forced abandonment of black children. Minny is the only black female domestic in the film that viewers see with her children. With them she is the disciplinarian providing them "tough love" as preparation for their eventual roles as servants to white folks.

The melodramatic stereotypical story of black female domestics and white employers told in *The Help* is no new story. The same filmic narrative entertained audiences in the 1950s when Douglas Sirk's tearjerker *Imitation of Life* came to the big screen. Just as the individual white woman in the film, played by actress Lana Turner, is depicted as a self-centered, self-serving bitch who cares only about her own personal fulfillment and who cannot be bothered to take care of her children, the black domestic who works for her is depicted as the long-suffering, caring embodiment of true maternal womanhood. Like an invisible back-up singer, the black female character's role is to call attention to the failings of white womanhood. The lead singer, the truly vital story, is that of white womanhood gone astray. Portrayed as perverse in both *Imitation of Life* and in the contemporary film *The Help*, white women always need and demand to be the center of attention. In both these films the horror story that compels audiences is never what is happening with black females but rather how the interaction between the two groups serves to graphically highlight the monstrous nature of white women.

According to the filmic narrative of *The Help*, it is not simply racism that has pitted white and black females against one another. Rather the film suggests it is the innate perverse nature of females to compete with one another; race just adds a spicier component to this natural order of things. Clearly, female competition for power and presence is the most potent narrative conveyed in *The Help*. Since advertising claims that the point of the film is to expose negative exploitative bonds between white female employers and black domestics, it is easy for audiences to ignore the extent to which the film actually gives most of its attention to creating a damning portrait of white womanhood. Throughout *The Help* almost all the white females are portrayed as ruthless and vicious not just toward the black help, but also toward anyone deemed powerless. Almost all the white women in the film are so hateful they cannot be bothered to love and care for their children. This is the real story Skeeter longs to expose. And it is her relationship with her mother, Charlotte, that best epitomizes the sadomasochistic bond between white women and their children.

Constantly nagging and shaming Skeeter in the name of love, Charlotte diminishes her daughter's self-esteem. And like Mae Mobley, who would be a tragic victim of soul murder were it not for the care Aibileen gives her, Skeeter's efforts to self-actualize are motivated by her nostalgic relationship with the caring black domestic Constantine. When Mae tells Aibileen that Aibileen is her "real mother," the film's insistence that white females are perverse and monstrous is underscored. Relationships between white mothers and their daughters in the film are all characterized by intimate terrorism.

Shaming is the weapon white women use to dehumanize the folks they want to dominate. This use of shame as a weapon is particularly present in the relationship between the dominating alpha female Hilly, who wields both race and class power over the "white trash" female Celia. It is not satisfying enough for Hilly to mock, ridicule, and shame Celia, her cohorts must join her in this persecution. Her hatred of Celia exemplifies the assertion Dorothy Allison makes in her essay "A Question of Class": "The horror of class stratification, racism and prejudice is that some people began to believe that the security of their families and communities depends on the oppression of others, that for some to have good lives there must be others whose lives are truncated and brutal." That racism and class elitism normalizes the exploitation and oppression of black folks as well as those who are considered "white trash" is highlighted in this manner.

By showing Celia's plight, all be it in a farcical and slapstick manner, the movie attempts to show audiences that class and race prejudice together can be used to effectively demonize powerless individuals. Concurrently shared suffered brings folks together. It serves as the basis for the friendship between Celia and Minny, the black maid who works for her. Ironically, Celia as white trash outsider is the one white woman in the film who refuses to embrace the white supremacist dictate that there should be no intimacy between black and white. She insists on intimacy.

Positively, Celia is portrayed as capable of a genuine sisterhood. She even dares to physically fight white male patriarchy in order to protect Minny. Skeeter, who is the symbolic example of a contemporary feminist, challenges the assumption that a woman needs a husband, daring to be adventurous and independent. But in her own way she is as narcissistic as the mean-spirited southern white women whose cruelty she wants to expose. Willing to sacrifice the well-being of black female domestics for her fame and glory, Skeeter is the empowered modern white woman, the iconic feminist. However at the end of the day she never offers her black female informants the sisterhood Celia offers Minny. Skeeter is all theory and no practice; she exemplifies the "false sisterhood" Laura Ingraham writes about when she critiques the combination of "opportunism, acquiescence and dependency" that accurately characterized some pseudo-feminist women, the women who want it all.

Ultimately the message the movie *The Help* conveys is not, as Kathryn Stockett declares in her own words that she hopes the novel will show, that there was "so much love between white families and black domestics." What is really shown is that there was so much hate during this time period, and in the end sisterhood did not change the nature of that hate. In the novel what Skeeter learns about Constantine is that she has been fired because her daughter, who passes for white, dares to enter Miss Charlotte's household through the front door and conduct herself as an equal, thereby giving lie to the notion that race makes folk different from one another. When the southern white women, members of the Daughters of the American Revolution (DAR), are chatting with Lulabelle they regard her as one of them because they do not know she is black. It is interesting to note that in the film Lulabelle's character is portrayed by a dark-skinned black female wig-wearing rude character. This cinematic fictive representation, like so much else in the film, shifts the focus away from racial identity and allows female cruelty to overshadow the critique of white suprema-cist notions of difference Stockett highlights and exposes in the novel with this scene. By changing these characters the film makes it appear that Skeeter's mother Charlotte is simply cruelly acting out of egotis-tical vanity and not out of fear that racial difference will be exposed as the social construction that it is.

In the wake of the many successes of the contemporary feminist movement, there has been tremendous backlash. One aspect of that backlash has been the continued sexist insistence that female solidarity is not really possible because women will always compete and betray one another. Even in feminist circles, when communication broke down and conflict ensued, voices could be heard expressing contempt for the concept of sisterhood. Within some feminist groups and in the larger society, books began to appear negating notions of shared sister-hood. Conflicts were especially negative involving mothers and daugh-ters. Throughout the movie *The Help,* catfights are the norm. They are especially mean-spirited when they occur between white mothers and daughters. While black females are busy preparing their daughters to be subservient to whiteness, white mothers torment their daughters. Audiences are not given any explanation for the hatred between Hilly and her mother. When professional white males say they "loved" the film, they reveal their delight in seeing the power-hungry ruthlessness of white women, their cruelty, their unkindness exposed.

Throughout the novel and to some extent in the film, there is an ongoing discourse about kindness. That narrative is primarily voiced by black females. Aibileen gives all her charges little mini-lectures about kindness. And all the black domestics determine a white woman's worth by the extent to which she treats those who are less powerful with kindness. To counter the maternal cruelty toward white children, especially Mae Mobley, Aibileen offers the counter-hegemonic vision of being kind. She tells children the "secret stories" that aim to instill them with anti-racism humanism. She tells Mae who calls herself "bad" that this is not so. She tells her, "You a kind little girl." And Aibileen ponders what will happen "if I told her she something good every day."

Talking with a group of women's studies professors, black and white, with whom I watched *The Help*, we all pinpointed the exaggerated number of catfights in the film as one of the scenarios that gave the movie its mass appeal. Audiences delight in seeing women torture, betray, and fight one another. It gives lie to any notion that females are morally and ethically better than males. There is no kinder, gentler white female in the film. Thus, the current spate of books which tell readers that sisterhood has failed. Books like *Not My Mother's Daughter* and *Twisted Sisterhood* document women's inhumanity to women. This is a patriarchal narrative, and it is no wonder that powerful white males find it compelling. It profoundly dehumanizes women.

Many academic black women critiqued *The Help*, both book and movie, for its ugly portraits of black womanhood, making compelling arguments like that of the Association of Black Women Historians who maintain that *The Help* "distorts, ignores, and trivializes" the real-life experiences of black domestic workers. This is a necessary critique, but it does not change those aspects of the book and film that offer positive stereotypes of black women. Despite the lack of historical accuracy and the over-the-top negative stereotypical images, black females are humanized in a way that white females are not. Practically every white woman in the film is depicted as lacking courage and character, as being without emotional intelligence. They are depicted as feral animals willing to destroy anyone, even their children, to achieve their own ends. What is most dangerous about these fictive representations is that they erase and deny the long and powerful history of the individual radical white women active in the civil rights struggle, both in anti-racist and feminist movements—white women whose contributions helped bring freedom and liberation. If one believed in outlandish conspiracy theories, it would not be difficult to assume that white female critique of imperialist white supremacist capitalist patriarchy, of white male power, is mocked in *The Help* by representations that suggest white women may not have been on the front lines of race, gender, and class exploitations and oppression, but they certainly acted out in daily life the brutal colonizing dominating mindset.

Despites evocations, especially through marketing strategies, which exploit the notion that solidarity between individual women prevailed in the segregated south, the overall message of this film is that most white women are disloyal to their men, to their children, to one another, and to women different from themselves. Ironically, despite years of exploitation and oppression, it is the long years of friendship between Aibileen and Minny, their care and respect for one another, that is the lasting positive connection between two women. Skeeter, like the real-life Kathryn Stockett, will go on her way toward pursuing her opportunistic goals, without so much as a "look back and see" at the lives of black women. Ironically, *The Help* was Stockett's nostalgic way to remember, only what she remembers and the way she tells her story in no way reveals her capacity to think and write from a non-biased anti-racist perspective. Luckily for her there exists an entire supportive public framework of imperialist white supremacist capitalist patriarchy both in the world of publishing and in the movie making business that was and is eager to use the fictive plantation culture she creates to increase the wealth of powerful white males. And, of course, the black actors who assume the minstrel positions offered them for pay, for fame, make them as crudely opportunistic as the author. Certainly, it mocks and trivializes the suffering black folk endured at the hands of white oppressors to turn this story into cinematic comedic entertainment.

Like many popular "animal house" productions, the filmic version of *The Help* uses much toilet humor to entertain audiences. It deploys comedy and farce to shift attention away from the brutal cruelty white supremacist segregation generated in the lives of southern white and black folk. Growing up in the south, I often heard black elders talk with deep disgust about the real-life animal house antics of white folks. Black female domestics in their role as organic anthropologists observing white folks in the intimacy of their homes often returned to segregated black worlds with many stories about food fights, about food waste, and about the scatological humor of white folks. That obscene humor is certainly present in *The Help.*

In no historical testimony I have read from does an individual black domestic give an account of black women cooks putting fecal matter in the food they served to dominating whites, as happens in *The Help.* Given the intimate terrorism and the exploitation suffered as a consequence of white supremacy no doubt black folks imagined a multitude of vengeful acts that would offer them a sense of justice, yet abject terror and fear of punishment made it all but impossible for them to act out these vengeful feelings. Audiences can only ponder why Stockett envisions the height of black resistance to racism being enacted by a black cook adding fecal matter to a chocolate pie. Surely this is the stuff of perverse racist fantasy. After showing the extreme subservience of black folk in the segregated south, it does make sense that such a visceral act of rageful resistance would realistically have taken place. For indeed the book and the film rub our noses in the insane notion of white supremacist folk being so concerned that the "diseased" black people not use the same toilets as themselves while allowing them to care for their babies and cook their food. Clearly, dominating whites were not fearful of black folks contaminating their food.

Both book and movie have generated much conversation about race and representation. Sadly, much of the discussion has been banal discourse about good and bad images, about stereotypes, about historical inaccuracy. Fiction need not strive for historical accuracy; however, it can indeed offer alternative and transformative visions. There is no imaginative new vision in *The Help*. When the chosen subject matter is race and gender, there is a profound need for representations that take audiences beyond overused stale stereotypes and conventions. It's the unconventional stories of white female employers and the black female domestics that worked for them that need to be told in fiction or non-fiction. Speaking of her past, of her relationship to Constantine, whom she has violently rejected to secure white supremacist standing and favor, the white woman employer Charlotte shares with her daughter: "They say it's like true love, good help. You only get one in a lifetime." These true love stories are not told in *The Help*. Those of us who long to hear and to tell the "secret stories" that celebrate true freedom, that offer us all a chance to know optimal well-being, can only hope that *The Help*, a truly poorly written book and an even more badly done movie, may serve as an intervention. It may make way for new and different stories to be told, stories that will take us to places we have not been before, empowering us so that we can re-imagine the past and invent positive futures.

6

Interrogating:
The Reinvention of
Malcolm X

Reading *The Autobiography of Malcolm X: As Told to Alex Haley* in my late fifties, I find it remains one of the most compelling stories of political awakening. I was in my first year of college when I was loaned the autobiography. On fall break and staying with affluent white friends, I read the autobiography and it left me speechless, it closed me off from my white friends as it forced me into an awareness of the social as well as the political dynamics of racism. The recent publication of Manning Marable's biography of Malcolm served as the catalyst for my re-reading of the autobiography after more than forty years. In the small world of black academics and intellectuals, anyone who knew Manning for long years knew that he was slowly working on what he hoped would be the "definitive" biography of Malcolm X.

Like Manning, every black academic I know who in any way identifies with leftist politics not only understands the importance of Malcolm as both an iconic representation of the black freedom fighter and also as a fierce proponent of black self-determination. Indeed the foundation of my political awakening in my late teens was firmly established when I both completed the autobiography and learned from reading it other books that I should read. Were I called upon to pinpoint mentor figures who taught me how to be a critical thinker, how to make necessary observations and ask relevant questions, Malcolm X would be dutifully named. Most importantly I learned from reading about the life of Malcolm X, through later interviews and speeches, that it was important for a revolutionary thinker to be willing to admit mistakes, learn from them, and move forward. In his concluding chapter to the Prologue that sets the tone of his biography, Marable, who has already emphasized that Malcolm X made many mistakes, tells readers: "But unlike many other leaders, Malcolm had the courage to admit his mistakes, and even to seek and apologize to those he had offended. Even when I have disagreed with him, I deeply admire the strength and integrity of his character." This declaration seems both ironic and somewhat hypocritical as there is a consistent emphasis in Manning Marable's *Malcolm X: A Life of Reinvention* on Malcolm X's mistakes, all revealed by the biographer in a manner reminiscent of a celebrity tabloid exposé.

Certainly Marable, working for years with many research assistants, has managed to offer to the world a seriously pedantic biography of Malcolm X that is loaded with facts. However, sprinkled throughout the ostentatious compilation of hard facts are strange gossipy speculations. There is much seemingly pointless speculation about Malcolm X's personality and private life. This is especially the case as it pertains to issues of sexuality and sexual relationships. For example, writing about Malcolm X's marriage to Betty Shabazz, Marable shares: "In Malcolm's telling (and in Spike Lee's film), sexual attraction was the primary force drawing the two together, yet some of those who worked closely with Malcolm saw things differently. James 67X recalled that the minister saw his marriage as the fulfillment of an obligation to the Nation." The reader does not know what to make of this information since there is no evidence offered to support the notion that Malcolm was swept away by sexual lust. If this was how he described the seductive forces leading him into marriage then where is the evidence to confirm Malcolm's "telling"? There are many such moments like this in the book, where sly, negative allusions are made concerning Malcolm's sexuality without any corroborating facts—something which appears odd in a biography that is so given over to presenting a catalogue of hard facts.

Throughout his book Marable constantly references, in a somewhat mocking manner, the many changes in thought and perspective Malcolm X made throughout his life. Ironically, the change that is most surprising to many readers acquainted with the author is his shift from creating a work that was initially aimed at revealing more about Malcolm's politics and leadership toward creating a work that fixates on personality in a manner that not only depoliticizes but also represents Malcolm X, more often than not, as mere shrewd con man opportunist. While Marable has produced a biography strong in documentary facts, it is the speculative moments that undermine this work, especially his reliance on the cult of personality. Whether he intended it to be so or not, the overall effect is one that depoliticizes Malcolm X by presenting his political choices as emerging not from a moral and ethical foundation of critical thinking and careful reflection but rather solely from an opportunist trickster sensibility.

In setting the stage for what will follow, Marable, in the prologue "Life Beyond the Legend," tells readers that Malcolm was "a product of the modern ghetto." Marable contends: "The emotional rage he expressed was a reaction to racism in its urban context: segregated urban schools, substandard housing, high infant mortality rates, drugs, and crime." And even though Malcolm declared: "I know nothing about the South, I am a creation of the Northern white man," this was mere hyperbolic rhetoric. Superficial interpretations of Malcolm X's politicization make it appear that the experience of southern black folks in confronting extreme racist apartheid and its

concomitant oppression and exploitation had no significant impact
on his consciousness. Since most of the black folks living in the urban
ghetto who had southern roots migrated north to leave behind brutal
racist oppression, it is unlikely that Malcolm would not have heard
their woes mingled with rage about how the north had not proven to
be a safer, more progressive place. Although he was not coming from
the south, Malcolm X migrated north for similar reasons, and almost
all of those reasons involved flight, a turning away from traumatic
experiences toward the hope of building a new and better life. This
intermixing of varied geographical and cultural black experiences is
brilliantly documented in Isabel Wilkerson's important book on black
migration, especially on the movement of black folks to northern
cities, *The Warmth of Other Suns*.

Since Marable does not use any particular psychological model
as a paradigm by which Malcolm's shifts in perspective, growth in
awareness, and struggles for self-actualization might be understood,
he can only represent these changes as the machinations of a twisted,
disordered, grandiose ego. As an abuse survivor, a victim of family
dysfunction, societal abuse, and abandonment by chosen kin, it fits
that Malcolm X would use tools of survival learned early on—being
hyper-vigilant, bonding with authority figures and protectors, trusting
no one—in his adult life. When Malcolm X first talked with Alex
Haley he shared: "My whole life has been a chronology of changes."
Keeping this in mind, it is truly disturbing to have both Manning
Marable and other anti-Malcolm X critics act as though Malcolm's
openness to change was somehow a constant opportunistic ploy.
Marable even casts suspicion on the transformative experience
of Malcolm X's journey to Mecca suggesting that Malcolm only
"appeared to experience a spiritual epiphany." Further stating his
case against Malcolm X, Marable writes: "He visited the holy city
of Mecca on a spiritual hajj, and on returning to the United States
declared that he had converted to orthodox Sunni Islam. Repudiating
his links to both the Nation of Islam and its leader, Elijah Muhammad,

he announced his opposition to all forms of bigotry. He was now eager to cooperate with civil rights groups, he said, and to work with any white person who genuinely supported black Americans." Since it was the telling of Malcolm X's post-pilgrimage transformation in Alex Haley's autobiography that most impresses many readers, Marable utterly undermines the power of this narrative when he writes as though this was just another strategic manipulative move on Malcolm X's part to garner greater power and fame.

Certainly, Marable's insistence throughout the biography that it was Alex Haley's *Autobiography of Malcolm X* that elevated Malcolm's power is an accurate interpretation. However, Marable does not paint a full picture when he suggests that Malcolm's impact was primarily felt by "black urban mid-century America." As a southern girl reading the *Autobiography*, I was entranced by Malcolm's process of politicization. His coming to critical consciousness sparked a mirroring experience in many readers, myself included. Growing up in the world of southern racist apartheid, I, like so many black folks, had been schooled in the art of acceptance and submission to white authority. Tamping down all rage and the concomitant will to resistance was the norm. Malcolm X gave readers of the *Autobiography* permission to revolt, to express rage, and to see anger at injustice as a constructive catalyst for radical politicization. While the stories of Malcolm X's "gangster years," his glorified criminal activities, his outspoken sexism and misogyny (expressed at a historical moment when feminist liberation struggle was garnering major momentum) gave colorful backdrop to his life story, it was not these stories that were deeply emotionally compelling; it was the gripping confessions of coming to political awareness and transformation. It was the recognition of Malcolm's love of justice and his sincere longing to create a better life for black folks.

My generation (folks born in the fifties) who were moving from grave circumstance of racist exploitation and oppression, who were living the experience of racial apartheid in the United States— whether in the small town south or in large cities—were galvanized by Malcolm X's life story. And dare I say it, few readers were so enamored of his tales of personal exploits that we did not recognize possible moments of hyperbole and even misrepresentation. Marable sees the contemporary fascination with the iconic Malcolm X that surfaced among young black folks in popular culture (movies, films, clothing) as furthering the legend. In his long *New Yorker* essay, white journalist David Remnick reminds readers that the *Autobiography* sold six million copies worldwide and "the book continues to sell briskly." Clearly, interest in Malcolm X continues.

In the acknowledgments and research notes at the end of *A Life of Reinvention,* Marable confesses that it was the moment when he "finally realized that critical deconstruction of the *Autobiography* held the key to interpreting Malcolm's life" that he had found his platform. Ultimately, it is Marable's desire to deconstruct the *Autobiography* that weakens the biography because it leads to exaggerated emphasis on matters that tell us little about the man behind the legend. Marable's obsession with exposing the misrepresentations and flaws of the *Autobiography* lead him to engage in little or no meaningful interpretation of material. For example: he depicts Malcolm X as being unloving towards his wife. Readers are made privy to the details of their unsatisfying sex life. Yet, we are left with no clear insight as to how sexuality shaped Malcolm's identity and his politics.

Since Manning Marable, who had been battling a life-threatening illness for years, died shortly before the biography reached the public, readers cannot interrogate him about his intention or strategy. Most reviews of the book have been positive. And indeed, despite Malcolm's many fans and followers, the press seemed to welcome and applaud a work that demeans Malcolm X's life and politics. Certainly, the huge amount of attention this biography has received tells the public that when it comes to the press, Malcolm X still has more enemies than friends. In his December speech at the Audubon, Malcolm X warned listeners about the power of the conservative press, declaring: "that someone can take a newspaper and build an image of someone so that before you even met them you'll run…all you know is what the press has had to say and the press is white. And when I say that the press is white, I mean it is WHITE. And it's dangerous." Certainly, the youth sub-culture that has throughout the years since Malcolm X's death claimed him as icon and mentor must now confront a white-dominated mainstream press that is symbolically assassinating their hero once again. Even though African American pop culture evokes the image and words of Malcolm X so much so that polls show that eighty-four percent of African Americans between the ages of fifteen and twenty-four revere him, these young folk are not the buyers that marketing for Marable's book has targeted. The press that has pushed Marable's book and claimed it to be definitive has pitched this work as a tell-all exposé that will reveal the man behind the mask and expose to the world that Malcolm X was more trickster con artist than astute political observer when it came to the politics of race both at home and abroad.

Shortly before his death, as he saw himself misrepresented in media, Malcolm declared: "The press is so powerful in its image making role, it can make a criminal look like he's the victim and make the victim look like he's the criminal. This is the press, an irresponsible press.…That's the image making press. That thing is dangerous if you don't guard yourself against it." Certainly, it is the *white* press that has hyped Marable's book, using the occasion of its publication to spread the word that Malcolm X was in truth "nobody's hero." Given the rise in fascism globally and the rise in the white supremacist right in the United States, there are few revolutionary fronts. Yet all over the world, young people are the militant radical protestors calling for justice, for freedom, for an end to domination. For many of these new freedom fighters, Malcolm X remains the heroic figure, the mentor. Consequently, it is in the interest of conservative white power to insist on projecting the image of Malcolm X as imposter, con man, opportunist. Clever advertising and marketing, especially reviews, of Marable's biography, make this work the perfect backdrop to enact a current symbolic assassination of Malcolm X.

It was the press that announced to the public that Marable's work would reveal heretofore unknown facts about Malcolm's life—facts, of course, that would show the world that Malcolm X was an imposter. One of these so-called facts was Marable's assertion that he had found evidence proving that Malcolm X was a homosexual. No distinction is made between a man who engages, as apparently Malcolm X did, in one homosexual relationship and a man who has a consistent homosexual sexual practice. Any long-time follower of scholarship about Malcolm X would know that white male scholar Bruce Perry had revealed this one homosexual relationship in his 1991 biography of Malcolm X. At that time the mainstream press showed little interest in Perry's revelations, and black critics simply denounced him. To any astute observer, it came as no surprise that in his hedonistic days of living on the edge, of poverty, substance abuse, and debauchery, that Malcolm X would engage in a homosexual relationship, one that was primarily an exchange of sex for money.

If any body of facts exists that proves Malcolm X was a closeted homosexual, it would indeed be a meaningful revelation. But when Marable implies on one hand that Malcolm X was gay and on the other hand that it was his sexual passion for an early heterosexual love that led to his leaving the Nation of Islam or that his "supposed" relationship with a girl in her late teens triggered his marital conflict, it is clear that the idea of Malcolm X as gay was simply an exaggeration, aimed at drawing attention to Marable's book. Bruce Perry was discredited when he asserted that Malcolm X had a homosexual encounter.

Malcolm X's wife, Betty Shabazz, was one of the most outspoken critics of Perry's work. When I referred to Perry's account of Malcolm's homosexual experience in her presence, she accused me and the biographer of attempting to slander her husband. Like Malcolm X and Marable, Shabazz has passed away and is unable to rise from the dead to interrogate all the ways the current conservative press is creating a new demeaning image of her husband. Brutal descriptions of the negativity in their marriage are part of this new sexualized discourse.

Documents that indicate Shabazz's dissatisfaction with Malcolm X as a sexual partner add weight to the covert implications that he was really a homosexual.

Conservative critics, white and black, who dwell on Malcolm's sexuality aim to depoliticize him by slyly suggesting that he was just another brother on the down low (i.e., posing as straight, screwing females to cover up his homosexual appetite). Since much African American youth-based pop culture mirrors the homophobic values of this imperialist white supremacist capitalist patriarchal society, to inform this group that their "shining black prince" was really a queen in disguise is a character assassination aimed at both promoting homophobia while simultaneously encouraging this group to denounce Malcolm X, to no longer see him as a champion of black manhood but as an enemy. If this is accomplished, Malcolm X's life and experience will no longer serve as the catalyst for youth of all ages and all colors to come to critical consciousness and radical politicization.

When talking with young students, I experience firsthand the way in which the press projecting the image of Malcolm X as a homosexual on the down low creates havoc. Here is one example reported to me during office hours: a black female student who came out as gay to her single mom while simultaneously gaining critical consciousness via her study of Malcolm's life and work was interrogated by her mother (who had read in the press that he was gay) as to whether her interest in Malcolm X had "made her gay." As some observers have done with Malcolm X's life story, this young woman's mother chose to focus on her daughter's sexuality instead of her daughter's engagement with critical thinking and radical politics. Of course, no writer who has fixated on Malcolm X's sexuality has theorized what it would mean both in our understanding of his life and leadership had he indeed been a homosexual. Certainly the profound sexism and misogyny expressed throughout much of his adult life is much more typical of patriarchal heterosexual learned behavior. Had Malcolm chosen to claim a gay identity, it would no doubt have aided him in transforming his attitudes toward the female gender. And while it is sensational and provocative to imagine Malcolm X morphing from "shining black prince" into fierce fabulous queendom, the facts merely document conflicted sexual practices. Indeed, when we finally do have a definitive biography of Malcolm X, one that not only brings forth well-documented facts but one that dares to interpret those facts using the tools of both sociology and psychology, the world might truly begin to know this charismatic leader. Every mindful and aware observer who would understand Malcolm must honestly know that he was flawed, that he was not perfect. But who among us would want to be known solely by our failings? The most important lesson I learned from studying the life and work of Malcolm X was the importance of self-actualization through critical vigilance, a radical openness that would allow one to admit mistakes, to grow and change.

Sadly, Manning Marable's biography does not really aid readers in fully understanding the man behind the legend. More importantly, the way this biography has been used and will be used to serve the interests of imperialist white supremacist capitalist patriarchy's continued racist/sexist assault on black masculinity should remind us all that the struggle for black self-determination must be ongoing. Indeed it is a matter of life and death. Everyone, individuals of all colors, who found or will find their way to freedom's struggle by following Malcolm X, by learning from his life and work, must play a role in protecting that which is meaningful and empowering about his legacy. That means we must rigorously interrogate sources of information. We must not allow a cult of celebrity to continue to shape the future image of Malcolm X. Let us remember his passion for justice, his prophetic call for continued resistance: "I'm not against somebody because of their race, but I'm sure against them because of what they're doing; and if they're doing wrong, we should stop them, and by any means necessary."

7

Tragic Biography: Resurrecting Henrietta Lacks

In the first book I wrote and published more than twenty years ago, *Ain't I a Woman: Black Women and Feminism,* I included a chapter entitled "Continued Devaluation of Black Womanhood," in which I declared that "a devaluation of black womanhood occurred as a result of the sexual exploitation of black women during slavery that has not altered in the course of hundreds of years." Emphasizing the reality that unenlightened black females often embrace stereotypes that depict us as strong matriarchs I contended: "Once black women are deluded and imagine that we have power we don't really possess, the possibility that we might organize collectively to fight against sexist-racist oppression is reduced." At the time of this early feminist writing, I interviewed a black woman usually employed as a clerk who was living in near poverty, yet she continually emphasized the fact that the black woman was "matriarchal, powerful, in control of her life." Actually, she was on the edge of a nervous breakdown, daily struggling just to make ends meet. I wrote then: "Without a doubt, the false sense of power Black women are encouraged to feel allows us to think that we are not in need of social movements that would liberate us from sexist oppression." Since I first wrote these words individual and collective groups of black women have struggled to be self-defining, to invent identities for ourselves that are acts of resistance challenging negative stereotypes—those racialized sexist projections imposed upon us—while simultaneously working to create foundations for self-actualization and self-determination.

Despite tremendous efforts to change the overall way black women are regarded in imperialist white supremacist patriarchal capitalist culture, there is no black woman, no matter how liberated, who does not encounter on some level in daily life efforts on the part of dominator culture to restrict her freedom, to force her into an identity of submission. In *Killing the Black Body: Race, Reproduction, and the Meaning of Liberty,* law professor Dorothy Roberts continually emphasizes that it is essential for black women to participate fully in critical discussions of liberty. Urging us not to abandon the discussion, she insists that "affirming the constitutional claim to personhood is particularly important to Black women because they have historically been denied the dignity of their full humanity and identity." Furthermore, Roberts explains: "The concept of personhood embodied in liberty can be used to affirm the role of will and creativity in Black women's construction of their own identities. Relying on the concept of self-definition celebrates the legacy of Black women who have survived and transcended conditions of oppression. The process of defining one's self and declaring one's personhood defies the denial of self-ownership inherent in slavery." Visionary feminist theory and practice focusing on the interconnectedness of race, class, and gender in conjunction with black liberation struggles have promoted black female self-determination. Yet all our progressive changes have not eliminated the continued devaluation of black womanhood.

Ironically, we now face a more formidable obstacle: the women and men of all races who exploit issues of race and gender for self-centered opportunistic concerns. Had there been no movements of black liberation, had there been no feminist movement, it is not likely that much of the academic work focusing on race and gender would have gained a hearing. These movements created the cultural climate both in the academy and elsewhere where work of this nature could and can have a voice and be received. Increasingly, more often than not, producers of such work discount any relation to either political movements for social justice or to the unlearning of racism and sexism that provide everyone the opportunity to create work that is not biased, that no longer upholds and perpetuates the tenets of racism and sexism. More often than not when works focused on race and gender are created with no attention given to whether the perspective of the writer is anti-racist or anti-sexist, familiar negative stereotypes are simply reproduced and reinscribed.

Although there are many works that exemplify this trend, one of the most recent is science journalist Rebecca Skloot's exploration of the HeLa cells and the black woman from whose body the cells were taken. Skloot titles her work *The Immortal Life of Henrietta Lacks.* On the cover readers find this caption: "Doctors took her cells without asking. Those cells never died. They launched a medical revolution and a multimillion-dollar industry. More than twenty years later, her children found out. *Their lives would never be the same.*" Marketed as a sensational discovery, this work purports to tell the story of Henrietta Lacks. Yet it is less a true story of Lacks's life and more a work of sensational creative nonfiction. Truthfully, Skloot's work cannot offer a complete portrait, for far too little of the true story of Lacks's life is known. Despite Skloot's extensive investigation she was not even able to uncover the reasons a young black female born Loretta Pleasant became known as Henrietta Lacks.

Conjuring images of Henrietta Lacks, Skloot employs a novelistic style that mimics the work of black women fiction writers (for example,

Zora Neale Hurston) though nowhere in her work does she refer to any
writing by black females. While she shares with readers the fact that Henrietta was raised with her cousin David Lacks, she assumes a folksy novelistic persona as the means by which she offers her fictive interpretation
of their lives. Her accounts of their childhood bonding reads "Henrietta
and Day had been sharing a bedroom since she was four, so what happened next didn't surprise anyone: they started having children together."
As readers we do not know where this information comes from or why
inappropriate sexual behavior is reported nonchalantly as though it is a
mere accepted fact of black people's lives. Skloot consistently portrays
the black folks she interviews in a sentimental manner, one that tends
to evoke a folksy image of down-home black folks with no cares in the
world, what I call "the happy darky syndrome." Paradoxically, she merely
states that Henrietta Lacks suffered from venereal disease yet she in no
way places the exploitation of Lacks's black female body in the context of
child abuse, racism, sexism, and class exploitation.

By failing to offer a more complex interpretation, she falls into
the trap of reinscribing simplistic notions of black identity. We learn
from Skloot that Lacks liked to have fun, to dance, to paint her nails
(much is made of her nails). Rather than creating a humanized portrait of Lacks, Skloot frames Lacks in the usual racist and sexist ways
of "seeing" black females—flirtatious and loose, lacking knowledge
about her own body, and with little concern for what it takes to be a
responsible mother. After portraying Lacks as a kind of modern child-
like primitive, Skloot also projects onto Lacks the stereotypical strong
black woman image. Offering this account of Lacks receiving the
news that she has cancer, Skloot writes, "On February 5, 1951, after
Jones got Henrietta's biopsy report back from the lab, he called and
told her it was malignant. Henrietta didn't tell anyone what Jones said,
and no one asked. She simply went on with her day as if nothing had
happened, which was just like her—no sense upsetting anyone over
something she could deal with herself." Skloot narrates what Lacks
does after telling her husband and children that she needed to see the

doctor again: "The next morning she climbed from the Buick outside Hopkins again, telling Day and the children not to worry." The words Skloot puts in Lacks's mouth read: "Ain't nothin serious wrong…Doctor's gonna fix me right up." This stereotypically super-mama portrait nicely fits with the suggestion throughout the book that there was and is an almost "supernatural" power in Lacks's cells, which white medical professionals had named HeLa. Skloot declares: "HeLa cells grew much faster than normal cells, and therefore produced re-sults faster. HeLa was a workhorse: it was hardy, it was inexpensive, and it was everywhere." This language is not unlike that used by plantation owners to describe hardworking black slaves: it dehumanizes.

There are three narratives contained within the book *The Immortal Life of Henrietta Lacks.* One is the short simplistic biographical portrait of Henrietta Lacks; it resides in the background because there is simply not much information about her adult life, what she actually thought, what her values were, what motivated her actions. The second narra-tive is the biographical story of her daughter Deborah, which is more complete and provides more of the human interest in the narrative both because of her testimony about the family (everything she shares about her mother comes from other sources) and also because she is a fount of information when talking about everyone's responses to the revelation that Lacks's cells were taken without her consent and then used for much medical good. The most complex and compelling narrative in the book is the story of the HeLa. That story is the only heartfelt narrative in the book.

Skloot's passion and compassion clearly lie with the medical and science community. And like many other commentators, she is both willing to acknowledge that ethical questions were and are raised by the appropriation of Lacks's body and later the bodies of Lacks's family members without full disclosure, yet she continually suggests by her approach that what is most important is the benefit to medical sci-ence that came from the use of Lacks's cells. Skloot is basically silent when it comes to addressing issues of racism and sexism as systems that allowed experimentation with Henrietta's body. Indeed, Skloot paints a portrait of Lacks's family as simply wanting money, as simply unwilling to recognize the extent to which they were all complicit in making agreements without fully understanding the implications of their actions. On those rare occasions when family members raise the issue of racism, Skloot distances her work from this discussion using phrases like "they say," which imply that there is no real basis for the charge of racism.

Constantly, she frames any discussion of the issue of racism alongside exaggerated stories and myths about medical experiments on black bodies. Significantly, a discussion among the family she transcribes and reports is placed in a chapter called "Night Doctors," which emphasizes exaggerated fears and myths about the use of black bodies. Paragraphs like the following, which concern the author's attempts to meet with family members expose Skloot's biases: "All I knew about Sonny's brothers was that they were angry and one of them had murdered someone—I wasn't sure which one, or why." She then reports that Deborah tells her, "Brother gets mad when white folks come askin about our mother." Yet there is no suggestion ever on the part of the author that a legitimate reason for anger exists.

More often than not Skloot is condescending and patronizing in her treatment of family members. And while Deborah is Skloot's key informant—the voice she uses to legitimize her own ruthless excavation of the black female body—Skloot continually portrays Deborah as a crazy black woman bitch who must be put in her place. Significantly, after one "crazed" encounter where she is being interrogated about her positionality by Deborah, Skloot does not give an account of her project by offering meaningful explanations, but instead she informs readers about all the ways Deborah is out of control and violent. Reporting on one of their encounters she acknowledges: "Then, for the first time since we met, I lost my patience with Deborah. I jerked free of her grip and told her to get the fuck off me and chill the fuck out. She stood inches from me, staring wild-eyed again and for what felt like minutes.

Then, suddenly, she grinned and reached up to smooth my hair." This scenario evokes standard negative racialized sexist stereotypes of black womanhood.

Deborah becomes in this moment both the embodiment of the angry black bitch and the caring black mammy. Note that Deborah's violence is deemed "crazy" whereas Skloot's verbal abuse is portrayed as simply a form of self-protection. No doubt she includes a description of this encounter to let readers know that she is a tough white woman not willing to take any shit from the black folks she is mining to produce the treasure that will be her book and lead to her fame. By the time the book ends, Deborah and her words are evoked giving both permission and validation for Skloot's project. Readers are told that in response to Skloot's insistence that her mother will be immortal Deborah says: "But I tell you one thing, I don't want to be immortal if it mean living forever....But maybe I'll come back as some HeLa cells like my mother, that way we can do good together out there in the world." This statement acts as a symbolic exoneration of all the violation visited upon black female bodies in this book: prevailing narratives of rape, incest, abuse.

Even though we learn that Deborah is a sexual abuse survivor, no link is made by the author between this experience and the irrational emotional responses that erupt from Deborah's troubled consciousness. Aspects of her story are deeply tragic, including the longing of a child for her mother that cannot be satisfied. Her inner child is in a constant state of unresolved mourning. And while Skloot does a fairly decent job of telling the facts of Deborah's life story, she does not bring any psychological depth to her interpretation. To recognize fully the impact of repeated trauma in Deborah's life Skloot would have had to relinquish the colorful darky aspects of her sensationalized thriller.

Significantly, readers never hear a harsh interrogation of the medical professionals involved in the exploitation of Lacks's body. In regards to her discussion with Susan Hsu, a doctor who had worked on the HeLa cells, she shares: "When I explained to her that the Lackses thought she was testing them for cancer, and that they were upset about scientists using the cells without their knowledge, she was shocked." Further on she reports this response from Hsu: "I feel very bad. People should have told them. You know, we never thought at that time they did not understand." Consistent with the seemingly "neutral" reporting voice Skloot uses in discussion with medical and science professions, she does not ask Hsu who would have been responsible for fully informing both Lacks and then later her family. While Skloot expresses sympathy now and then for this family, her allegiance is firmly with science, with the huge lasting benefits that came from the harvesting and sharing of the HeLa cells.

Indeed, the story of the HeLa cells is fascinating. And it is obvious to anyone who knows Michael Rogers's 1976 article in *Rolling Stone* magazine that Skloot has appropriated this early work and made it popular by sensationalizing the issues of the cells. Rogers was the first investigative reporter to bring, as Skloot acknowledges, "the true story of Henrietta Lacks and her family" to the public. As she says, his story was "the first time the mainstream media had reported that the woman behind HeLa was black." Unlike Skloot, Rogers endeavored to be explicit in calling out the ways racism had informed the erasure of Lacks's identity. However his article did not reach the mass audience that Skloot's book has, with its clever framing and marketing of the story as a sensational true-life mystery thriller. No one can argue that Skloot works hard to bring to light facts about the life of Henrietta Lacks and her family. Her hard work is evident and worthy of praise. Sadly, however, this work is biased. The true stories interspersed throughout this narrative are merely a sensational backdrop and are overshadowed by the story of scientific experimentation on human bodies—dead and alive.

Much of the human interest story shared in Skloot's work is written in a melodramatic sentimental vein. James Baldwin hit the mark when he defined sentimentality as "the ostentatious parading of excessive and spurious emotion…the mark of dishonesty, the inability to feel." Ironically, the cover of Skloot's book reveals the primary agenda behind this work; it exposes the extent to which the purported intent of the book to bring Henrietta Lacks into greater visibility is false. The photographic image of Henrietta Lacks does not have center stage. Her image, in the upper left-hand corner of the book, is practically disappearing from the page. The cover has a collage-like quality and the black-and-white image appears as if it is cut out and pasted onto the more colorful all-encompassing image of cells. This cover reveals to anyone who studies it that Henrietta Lacks is not immortal, that she may or may not be remembered, but that her cells will always have presence; they will always receive attention and recognition.

In fact, given the power of imperialist white supremacist capitalist patriarchy to erase black history (think of all the years that Lacks's presence was erased, her experience buried and forgotten) it is still possible that Lacks will recede into invisibility. And while the author attempts to suggest that this kind of undisclosed experimentation is an aberrant occurrence, the many violations of black female bodies by medical experimentation has not ended. Even though it serves Skloot's purpose to present this story as rare and uncommon, it is not. Of course the story of the HeLa cells is an awesome rare occurrence, one that can easily fascinate readers. There is nothing sensational about the exploitation and violation of black female bodies; it is such a common occurrence that it does not shock. And now that her identity is fully uncovered Lacks enters the community of a collective body of black females whom the medical industrial complex has violated and disowned. Perhaps one day we will hear the story of Henrietta Lacks told from the perspective of an aware observer willing to examine fully, boldly, and honestly the way racism, sexism, and class exploitation together informed and shaped the true life story of Henrietta Lacks and her kin.

When any woman's history (especially a woman of color) that has been buried and forgotten comes to light, there is cause for celebration. Many readers celebrate the uncovering of Lacks's role in a medical revolution even as we lament the myriad ways she is written into history via sexist and racist defined personas. Just as she entered medical history naked with aspects of her personhood denied, bits of her body taken, and her name (therewith her story) buried, parts of her being are again violated when she is called a "thing" by Skloot, when what is written on her long dead body is another story of someone else's desire and passion—the science journalist who wants to reveal a story to the world that will bring her fame and glory. No one who is unable to assume an unbiased perspective informed by keen understanding of the way systems of imperialist white supremacist capitalist patriarchy have worked together—historically in Africa and in the United States from slavery to the present day—to deny life to the black female body can offer readers Lacks's true story.

Taught by these very systems that the black female body exists as a vessel to feed and aid the growth of others and not to nurture the self, one cannot find in Skloot's narrative of Henrietta Lacks a story where she is the subject of her longings and not othered or dehumanized by outsiders who long to make her body carry their hopes and dreams. It is both the world of sexism in black communities and racism in white communities that condones and supports the violation of Lacks's black female body. That this violation is passed on is evident by the traumas visited upon the body of her daughter, the motherless child Deborah.

Until we (and everyone) recognize the suffering of black women as a more important marker of identity than the ways that pain is manipulated and exploited to serve the needs of others, black females will not be empowered to cultivate a resiliency of mind, spirit, body, and heart that requires no cover-ups, no false personas. As Kevin Quashie declares in his study *Black Women, Identity, and Cultural Theory,* "To be loved, to be held, to remember…are each metaphors of selfhood; they mark a subject and articulate [a black woman's] function but also imagine and suggest an other who is engaged in the act of be-ing." What we hope for Henrietta Lacks is that she be remembered for her unrequited martyrdom.

The tragic aspects of her life and death are rendered no less painful and traumatic by the heroic medical revolution engendered by the HeLa cells. To honor Henrietta Lacks rightly we must allow her body and being a subjectivity that both stands apart, even as it enhances the story of HeLa. To allow this tragic biography to become mere colorful backdrop, subordinated to the story of HeLa, is to reinscribe the notion that what is most vital in the lives of black subjects is not how we live but how we influence and change the lives of white folks. To humanize fully Henrietta Lacks she must come back to center stage.

We must return to her the dignity that the forces of hatred and greed have stripped away. We must not allow the racism, sexism, and class exploitation which over-determined her fate to be ignored. As enlightened visionary feminist women who recognize the importance of feminist thought and practice, we read her story and weep. Let us celebrate and let us mourn. Let us remember and let us resist. We reclaim your humanity Henrietta Lacks. For us you will never be immortal; we do not require immortality to value you rightly. As we reclaim your story as our story, we make certain that you will not be forgotten.

8

A Path Away From Race: On Spiritual Conversion

Martin Luther King's divine calling was to preach. He preached with an artistry, a divinely inspired creativity, that was wondrous to behold. He could call masses of people to hear the word of God; the holy, holy, holy spirit emanating from him was awesome. King was a prophetic witness. Able to convert listeners, he not only made it possible for them to hear sacred teachings, he invited them to open their hearts and be transformed. One of King's favorite scriptures, taken from the book of Romans, admonished believers, telling them: "Be not conformed to this world but be ye transformed by the renewal of your mind that you may know what the will of god is." Prophet, preacher, man of God, seeker on the path of righteousness and right action, King meditated often on this scripture because he sought direct connection with the divine. He knew he was constantly in need of divine guidance. Willing to critically reflect, grow, and change, he wanted only to do God's will.

King was not an original thinker. Passionate about ideas, he was awed by the insights of original thinkers—especially the works of intellectual and/or visionary men of genius. Open-minded, willing to study and learn, King's personal magic resided in his ability to take complex ideas and break them down bit by bit, placing them in a vernacular form that rendered them accessible to the widest possible audience. Two of the men who most influenced his thinking were Mahatma Gandhi and Erich Fromm. Challenged by the seemingly miraculous power of Gandhi's mission to bring about social revolution that would improve everyone's chances of living a life of well-being with peace, joy, and healing through nonviolent resistance, King became a prophetic witness for peace. Explaining the influence of Gandhi, King writes in his powerful work *Strength to Love:* "I had come to see early that the Christian doctrine of love operating through the Gandhian method of nonviolence was one of the most potent weapons available to the Negro in his struggle for freedom." Nonviolent resistance had emerged as the technique of the movement, while love stood as the regulating ideal. In other words, Christ furnished the spirit and motivation while Gandhi furnished the method.

Fromm's book *The Art of Loving* provided the intellectual framework for King's spiritual awareness of love as a divine force uniting all life. Interviewed by Kenneth Clark and asked to talk about a love ethic King referred to Fromm: "Many of the psychiatrists are telling us now that many of the strange things that can happen in the subconscious and many of the inner conflicts are rooted in hate and so they are now saying 'love or perish.' Erich Fromm can write a book like *The Art of Loving* and make it very clear that love is the supreme unifying principle of life and I'm trying to say in this movement that it is necessary to follow the technique of nonviolence as the most potent weapon available to us, but it is necessary also to follow the love ethic." It was Fromm's work which aided King in his understanding "that the right kind of self-love and the right kind of love of others are interdependent."

There were two amazing conversion experiences in King's life, his transformation into a nonviolent resister and his call for a social revolution of values based on commitment to love as political praxis, a love rooted in spiritual commitment to the Divine. In his biography of Francis of Assisi, *Reluctant Saint,* Donald Spoto offers an insightful complex understanding of the meaning of conversion. Speaking about spiritual transformation, he shares: "Conversion is, then, a response to God, Who invites us to a state of complete freedom, away from everything that is hostile to His goodness and mercy....The call Jesus extended to his disciples...was a summons to acknowledge God's unconditional love of us as individuals; and it was an invitation to proclaim that love to the world by acts of caring, forgiveness and compassion for others, by refusing to demand one's prerogatives at the expense of others and by rejecting vengeance and reprisal....Seen in this light, conversion means not only a turning away from one's past but entrusting oneself to the unexpected, uncharted way into the incalculable future in which God comes to us....Conversion then becomes a radical and uniquely personal adoption of a new life." Any critical study of King's private life reveals that his decision to oppose the war in Vietnam, his radical stance on nonviolence, was the gesture of surrender to divine will that signaled the depths of his spiritual surrender.

It took many days and nights of prayer and soul searching, of King asking himself "how can I say I worship a god of love and support war" to transform his consciousness and his actions. Confessing that it was no easy decision to stand against the nation and oppose war, King declared in his historic 1967 address "A Time to Break Silence," "Some of us who have already begun to break the silence of the night have found that the calling to speak is often a vocation of agony, but we must speak." Because King united theology with working for social change, it has been easy for folks to overlook the extent to which he struggled to accept new ideas, new visions. While the American public is aware that King called us to love one another, relying on biblical scripture, it is absolutely essential that we understand the depths of his spiritual devotion, a dedication grounded in his acknowledgment of god's unconditional love and his awareness that god was calling him to proclaim that love to the world even at the risk of losing his life. This is why King so often emphasized in his sermons that he had made a choice to love, proclaiming in his speech "Where Do We Go from Here?": "I have decided to love. If you are seeking the highest good, I think you can find it through love. And the beautiful thing is that we are moving against wrong when we do it, because John was right, God is love. He who hates does not know God, but he who has love has the key that unlocks the door to the meaning of ultimate reality."

As early as 1956, speaking to the First Annual Institute on Non-Violence and Social Change, King shared his views on love, explaining them at great length, telling his audience that the "virtues of love, mercy, and forgiveness should stand at the center of our lives." Stating that "love might well be the salvation of our civilization," he urged listeners to see love as the force that should shape the nature and outcome of resistance struggle, telling them: "the end is reconciliation; the end is redemption; the end is the creation of the beloved community....It is this love which will bring about miracles in the hearts of men." King understood that many unenlightened white folks feared that if black people gained greater power they would violently retaliate against those who had oppressed them, hence his constant insistence that black people love our enemies.

A teenager when Martin Luther King's courage and charisma rocked this nation and the world, I admired his commitment to anti-racist struggle. However that commitment did not seem to my adolescent mind as worthy of undue regard. In our white supremacist town, where racial apartheid was the norm, all our leaders preached working for civil rights struggle. All our leaders preached the love of one's enemies. In my teens I was more mesmerized by the political resistance of black power militants. If we had to choose between Malcolm and Martin, my vote was definitely going to be for Malcolm. Yet when

I left my small town, entered predominately white communities and colleges, becoming more involved in activist struggles for freedom, it was to the writings of King that I turned for inspiration and wise counsel.

Like many Americans I read King's slim volume of sermons *Strength to Love,* first published in 1963, to give me hope. By then it was evident that King's vision that love was the most constructive way to create positive social change benefiting everyone was changing our culture. Motivated by our belief in a love ethic, masses of Americans worked in the late sixties and early seventies to unlearn the logic of domination and dominator culture. While militant black power struggle certainly helped bring about important social reforms it also produced a culture of despair because the support for violence and imperialism was a central component of that agenda. King's insistence on love had provided folk an enduring message of hope. Tragically, he did not live long enough to be an enlightened voice for self-love among black people. King focused so intensely on the project of ending white racist assault on black people that he did not develop further his thinking about the necessity of self-love. However, in *Strength To Love* he spoke directly to those advocates of patriarchal imperialist violence, be they white or black, when he stated, "The hardhearted person never truly loves....The hardhearted person lacks the capacity for genuine compassion....The hardhearted individual never sees people as people, but rather as mere objects or as impersonal cogs in an ever-turning wheel....He depersonalizes life."

Aware of the need to end domination globally King cautioned: "In an effort to achieve freedom in America, Asia, and Africa we must not try to leap from a position of disadvantage to one of advantage, thus subverting justice. We must seek democracy and not the substitution of one tyranny for another....God is not interested merely in the freedom of black men, and brown men, and yellow men; God is interested in the freedom of the whole human race." King's vision of redemptive love held the promise that both oppressor and oppressed could recover from the wounds of dehumanization. This is a vision not unlike

that taught to us during the Vietnam War by beloved Buddhist monk
Thich Nhat Hanh, whom King nominated for a Nobel Peace Price.

Just as I turned to King's writing in my early twenties to renew
my spirit, more than twenty years later I returned to this work as I experienced renewed spiritual awakening, an ever growing awareness of
the transformative power of love. Like King, I had been undergoing
a conversion, not in the conventional sense of a defining moment
of change, but rather conversion as a process, an ongoing project. As
I studied and wrote about ending domination in all its forms it became
clearer and clearer that politics rooted in a love ethic could produce
lasting meaningful social change. When I traveled the nation asking
folk what enabled them to be courageous in struggling for freedom—
whether working to end domination of race, gender, sexuality, class, or
religion—the response was love.

All over the world people working for peace and justice evoke
King's vision of a beloved community where people committed to
nonviolence would create a new social order based on justice and
love. This was King's prophetic vision. In the *Soul of Politics,* Jim Wallis
reminds readers that "the prophetic vocation is to challenge the old
while announcing the new.... The Biblical prophets always had a two-
fold task. First they were bold in telling the truth and proclaiming the
justice that is rooted in God.... But in addition to truth telling, the
prophets had a second task. They held up an alternative vision, they
helped the people to imagine new possibilities." King's vision of living
out lives based on a love ethic is the philosophy of being and becoming that could heal our world today. A prophetic witness for peace, an
apostle of love, Martin Luther King has given us the map. His spirit
lights the way, leading to the truth that love in action is the spiritual
path that liberates.

9

Talking Trash:
A Dialogue About
Crash

bell hooks with filmmaker Gilda L. Sheppard

I want to interrogate specific films that were marketed and critically acclaimed as progressive texts of race, sex, and class to see if the messages embedded in these works really were encouraging and promoting a counter-hegemonic narrative challenging the conventional structures of domination that uphold and maintain white supremacist capitalist patriarchy.

bell

James Baldwin was fond of saying that "sentimentality is the ostentatious parading of excessive and spurious emotion. It is the mark of dishonesty, the inability to feel."

Many people see *Crash* as a film which invokes deep pathos and feelings. Actually, it is a sentimental and melodramatic film in the classic mode of Hollywood.

Gilda

A classic Hollywood mode that generally has a narrative structure characterized by the construction of a goal-oriented protagonist or "hero." This hero is usually male and white and he alone must resolve a situation. The supporting actors are situated as functionaries in the plot to fulfill some semblance of redemption for the hero. When people of color are cast in many Hollywood narratives, they are often-times used as props that hold up this hero, therefore sealing and nor-malizing a system of ideas and practices of white supremacist capitalist patriarchy. The hero becomes the "great white hope" or savior.

This is evidenced historically with Edwin S. Porter's 1903 twelve-minute film adaptation of *Uncle Tom's Cabin,* where the first black character presented in the film, who was played by a white actor, became somewhat of a departure from the intent and character of the original novel by Harriet Beecher Stowe. Stowe's novel was not a counter-hegemonic text; however, she attempted to write her novel as an anti-slavery text intended to expose the brutalities and immo-rality of slavery. The text, however flawed, did manage to enliven dis-course for the abolition of slavery. In the film version, Porter's Tom hero was a childlike, unthinking, and happy slave. The film's message was clearly that slavery was not all bad; in fact, the enslaved "whistled while they worked," like Disney's 1946 character Uncle Remus. Por-ter's film was made at a historical time when W.E.B. DuBois declared in the 1903 publishing of *Souls of Black Folk* that the "problem of the twentieth century is the problem of the color line." This was also a time when lynching was pervasive throughout post-emancipation USA. Therefore, the portrayal of the unthinking "happy darkie" in Porter's film was a complement to the 1915 post–Civil War and

Reconstruction era film *Birth of a Nation,* by D. W. Griffith. This racist and pro-KKK film that portrayed black people as brutes who prey on white women and therefore need to be subdued, arrested, and killed was used to protect the constructed sanctity of segregation policies; and to inform newly arrived citizens to beware and to accept that segregation must be guarded by such vigilantes as the KKK.

Therefore, the characters constructed in media, particularly Hollywood, are not merely racist character constructions. They also inform and reflect social policies and issues that impact human and civil rights. Just as Jared Ball writes in Voxunion Print Media:

> Media are not merely television, radio, film, books, Internet, etc. These are the technologies that make media available. Such a definition discourages a proper understanding of media as societal symbols, definitions, norms and ideology all intimately linked to questions of who will hold power and how that power will be maintained.

Racist stereotypical portrayals are embedded and persistent in the classic Hollywood construction of the hero, particularly when black people and other representations of marginalized characters are cast. The film *Crash* is not a departure from reinscribing these stereotypical constructions.

bell

In *The Hero with a Thousand Faces,* Joseph Campbell shows how western culture really thrives on the classical myth of the hero. The classical hero triumphs over his fellow man. He has strength. His heroism must be recognized. He takes what he wants by force and dominates others. In *Crash,* Matt Dillon's character, Ryan, is cast as the hero. He is the only character who rises above personal limitations, personal prejudices. His willingness to risk his life to save the life of a black woman he has violated and humiliated springs not from a concern for her humanity but rather from his desperate need to prove he is worthy of the status of hero. It is his moment of glory. And like all Hollywood heroes he steals the limelight. His sins are forgiven and he is allowed to continue his domination over others.

Viewers may not consciously experience the film as yet another film in a long line of racialized Hollywood narratives from *Birth of a Nation* to present-day films in which the themes and plots are centered on white male triumph over bestial emotions. We may not be conscious of that narrative, but it is playing itself out in the unconscious. It is the film narrative audiences have come to expect.

Gilda

This expectation has its impact on our sense of agency and critical inquiry. As you have written, "Whether we like it or not, cinema assumes a pedagogical role in the lives of many people. It may not be the intent of the filmmaker to teach audiences anything, but that does not mean that lessons are not learned....Movies not only provide a narrative for specific discourses of race, sex, and class, they provide a shared experience, a common starting point from which diverse audiences can dialogue about these charged issues." However, with few exceptions, the dialogue about *Crash* from media literacy corners, professors, educators, scholars, and activists has been dominated by congratulations for the film's bravery in tackling charged issues. It is infrequently questioned for its reinscription of a Hollywood narrative that perpetuates stereotypical images and conservative characterizations of issues involving race, class, gender, sexuality, and notions of empire—in other words, for its reinscription of white supremacist capitalist patriarchy. Using what you call the "oppositional gaze," the film warrants such an interrogation.

Having the police officer Ryan (Damon) as the only character in *Crash* whom the audience is allowed to view as dynamic is not at all discussed as a charged issue in the film. What is commonly stated is that "there are no heroes." This notion persists even when the audience is given an understanding of the reasons for Ryan's actions as being the human frailties of frustration and anger. We are constantly reminded in several scenes of his compassion for his ailing father. This compassion is carefully juxtaposed with the "contradiction" of his actions of sexual violations and his final and sudden triumph as the rescuer of the same black woman he sexually violated. No other character in *Crash* is constructed with such dynamism.

In fact, Ryan is presented as the compassionate son of an ailing father who suffers from a urinary tract infection. This is represented several times in the film through scenes of Ryan assisting his father, embracing his father in the bathroom, on the toilet no less. Ah, the penis factor as a symbol of manhood—this time, the fallen man! We learn that Ryan's father owned a janitorial business and hired black men at "decent wages"; however, Ryan states that his father lost contracts to minority contractors. This is what happens when you do liberal acts. You lose even your career and "manhood," and you will be exposed for all to see. This context becomes a scaffold in the film for the anti–affirmative action lines that are supported through an unscrupulous black police chief who consciously backs down when told about the actions of a racist police officer on his team. The black police officer actually states that he will not put his career "on the line" for "integrity" or "pursuit of justice." This scene levels the system of racism to an individual compliance from members of the oppressed group. In another scene, the subtext is clearly that affirmative action policies allow for unqualified hires, particularly based on race. The scene is ushered in by a black woman manager at a bureaucratic HMO who, with a name none other than Shiniqua, cannot or will not assist Ryan.

What is to be noted is that this scene is the first time the audience is introduced to the Ryan character. Ryan is introduced as he talks with Shiniqua, played by Loretta Devine. Perhaps director Paul Haggis received his cue from Bill Cosby, giving the character a name like Shiniqua as a code for ignorance. The facial antics of Shiniqua were choreographed to make buffoonery of so-called black expressions, recalling the caricatures found in minstrelsy, and thus providing a platform for the Ryan character to throw insults and express little surprise in his inability to receive help for his father from Shiniqua, who, because of her name, is of little surprise to him black and most certainly ignorant and unqualified to assist him.

Immediately after this encounter with one black woman, Shiniqua, Ryan's next action is to sexually violate another black woman during a bogus traffic stop of an upper-middle-class couple: Cameron, played by Terrence Howard, and the victim of violation, Christine, played by Thandie Newton. This bogus stop happens in spite of protests from Ryan's police partner, Hansen. Hansen is introduced in several scenes in the film as a liberal white police officer who speaks up whenever he sees violations against black people, and who is, like Ryan's father, an alleged "friend of Negro people." However, notably, the liberal Hansen in the end commits the only killing in the film. And, of course, as in the classical Hollywood form, it is of a black man. So, if you are liberal you might lose your "manhood," and you cannot be trusted because your innate fear of the other might cause you to suddenly kill. Having a black man among the first or as the only person to die in this film is another classic Hollywood film trait.

Ryan's actions of rabid sexual violation during the bogus traffic stop appear to be a reaction, albeit gross, to his encounters with two black women: first, his failed attempt to get assistance from Shiniqua for his ailing father, and secondly, Christine, who verbally protests his bogus stop and also comments that because of her light skin Ryan must have "thought he saw a white woman blowing a black man." Once again the mouth of a black woman is the object of terrorism against her. Ryan, therefore, must punish and tame her, as her African American TV director husband Cameron, as well as Hansen, both look on as powerless voyeurs. This public display of powerlessness allows them to be compliant in the face of white supremacist capitalist patriarchy, yielding to the subtext that there is nothing, absolutely nothing, one can do even if s/he outnumbers the agents of white supremacy. Verbal or physical protest is impossible.

What is worth noting is the sexualized cinematic direction by director Paul Haggis of both the sexual violation of Christine and then, the next morning, of the melodramatic rescue of Christine from a car crash. The white pornographic gaze in the direction of these scenes is clearly represented.

This is no fast and furious violation. The director carefully staged it in a medium close-up of Ryan's slow and calculating violation of Christine. Displaying Ryan's facial expression of pornographic pleasure as he stoops, the camera then follows his hands as they slowly move under Christine's dress and display a slightly jerking movement to indicate that he even penetrates her with his hand in his pornographic investigation of her body. The camera cuts to Christine's face, reduced from confident protest to pain and shameful submission. The camera focuses on Ryan's gaze as he speaks in low tones to Christine's husband about breaking the law by performing the lewd conduct of oral sex while driving. This reminds the viewer that the Thandie Newton character was introduced as not just a middle-class woman driving home with her husband, but that we suddenly see her head as she rises from giving her husband head while driving. First impressions are lasting? After the couple is allowed to leave, Christine receives little or no comfort from her husband. He later chastises her for talking her mouth off, as did Ryan, with sexual violation. Her husband says with a bit of rage, "What was I to do? They had guns." She turns her rage to her husband and decides not to even call in a complaint of the violation.

Soon after these scenes and suddenly, in cinematic time, the next morning the sexual violator Ryan performs a similar act of sexualized invasion, only this time it is seen as a rescue, a la the great white hope, of the character Christine from a dramatic car crash. This second time

Ryan encounters Christine she is screaming and vulnerable, pinned upside down in her car, barely breathing as he approaches her, telling her to calm down when she screams at the sight of him after recognizing him as her violator. She is once again vulnerable and helpless as Ryan says, "I am not going to hurt you," taking time to pull her dress down as if to protect his property and posit it as purity, as if to say, "I am not going to violate you this time. However, I am still the one in control." Yeah, I will save your pitiful ass because I am now transformed into the great white hope. Haggis again directs this rescue carefully as a sexualized scene, only this time Ryan tames Christine and she is finally compliant.

Ryan and Christine's lips nearly brush each other as she screams. The camera angles place them in prone sexualized positions as he jerks her seat belt open to unleash her from the overturned car. What is interesting is that the same background music, a bit angelic and heavenly, is the score for both scenes of violation and rescue. Once rescued and dragged from the soon-to-explode car, the final action in these scenes has Christine walking away from the accident with assistance from police and medics, and she suddenly turns to gaze at her "rescuer." This gaze is reminiscent of the scene from *Monster's Ball* when Halle Berry turns and gazes at Billy Bob Thornton while he aggressively fucks her from behind. These are not interrogating gazes. They give the impression that both female characters are saying, "I am grateful to you, my benevolent dictator." After this gaze the camera turns to Ryan kneeling on one knee looking at Christine as she is led away. His image overpowers the shot. Everything else is reduced to nothing, just as his image is larger than life. In this leap of faith "rescue," the audience is able to see an artifice of his psychological development in the narrative structure of the film.

bell

The film is seductive to audiences at this historical moment, because many black people feel that our voices and images, our pain, our suffering as caused by white supremacist exploitation and oppression are being ignored. Black viewers were moved by the fact that someone would take the time to portray the sense of violation we so often feel when confronting everyday racism. When the white cop stops the black couple, a symbolic lynching occurs. There is castration. There is public shaming and emasculation of the black man, not only by the white cop but also by the black woman. These are the same old stereotypical images. And ultimately, black women are blamed for black degradation, for putting the black male down. The one black female who is "together" is totally allied with whiteness and white male power. In the late 1960s and early 1970s, the question was who will be raised to revere the black woman? *Crash* tells us no one will ever revere the black woman because the black woman is not worthy to be revered. Thandie Newton's character as the biracial beauty epitomizes the female body that is the meeting place for black and white male desire, bringing another motif from slavery to the present day. She is the elegant leading lady, the lady of mutual desire, but she too is unworthy.

Like the stereotypical mulatto character Sarah Jane in the film *Imitation of Life,* her heroic moment comes when she is facing death. The Thandie Newton character, Christine, becomes the total tragic mulatto when she is able to "forgive" her sexual violator and surrender to his saving touch. She begs the white male to save her and clings to him.

Contrasting *Crash* as a public narrative about race with the film *The Bodyguard,* audiences would be able to see the difference between public open affirmation of white male regard for black women and the dehumanizing rituals that take place in *Crash.* In *The Bodyguard,* there is a scene with a white woman who comes between the Kevin Costner character and the Whitney Houston character, the black woman he desires. He lets this white woman know: I am not choosing you. He does not degrade the black female he cares about. Interestingly, in *Crash,* the Thandie Newton character must be reduced to this demeaning dehumanized mess, pleading with the white man to save her. He then becomes the Christ-like figure. The image of her crying, clinging to the white male, appears on many posters and advertisements for the film.

Rather than depicting her as an equal, as in *The Bodyguard,* we get the erasure of that liberating interracial narrative and the substitution of an interracial narrative where the black woman is always subordinated, dependent on the white male for her survival. No matter how beautiful Newton's character looks at the beginning of the film, that moment when she is clinging to the white man in her baptism by fire she looks monstrous. Her features are distorted. Ironically, it is only this time we see her being emotionally caring in her relationship with her black husband. Soon after this scene she calls and says, "I love you." We wonder what such love means in the context of all the betrayals we see in this film. In real life, the bodies of black females are not saved by heroic white male fascists.

In contemporary culture, the bodies of all those black women abandoned and lost, disappeared and dead in the wake of Hurricane Katrina, let the world know that the black female body is not worthy of salvation. It is an image of genocide. A disturbing aspect of *Crash* is the fake narrative of white male redemption of black woman-ness. In fact, the film overall is about how black woman-ness is destroyed and degraded. We see how black men and women are set up to be the agents of their own and each other's destruction while the white family is completely idealized. Even the Hispanic man in *Crash* is shown as having a tension-filled relationship with his wife. The message conveyed is that she is not his equal. He is the parenting person, the authority. Patriarchy is intact. *Crash* offers the image of white men as tolerant and compassionate and white women as weepy, unhappy, blundering idiots. The white woman is, in a sense, the continuation of the Victorian idea of the mad woman in the attic. Yet, she is still worthy of respect, whereas black people in this film get no respect. I am startled when black people tell me that *Crash* talks about race in a new and different way. It simply does not. One of the greatest films of our time to lead into a profound discussion about race is Spike Lee's *Four Little Girls*. This film has no raw sexuality, no raw contempt, no construction of nigger as beast. In *Crash,* the images of black people are poorly executed clones of the images of blackness depicted in Quentin Tarantino's film *Pulp Fiction* and in black exploitation films.

Crash begins with sexuality and sexuality is always racialized in America. The white male is portrayed as a voyeur looking into the bedroom of a black man and woman (in this case, the car is the symbolic bedroom).

Gilda

The editing and sequencing of the scenes in the film clearly illustrate a hierarchy of character development.

Structuring the sexual violation immediately after Ryan's failed conversation with Shiniqua is an attempt to set the audience up to view his actions as merely a contradiction of his character or, at best, to view his behavior as a reaction to feelings of misplaced anger that could be resolved in a few sessions of anger management. This narrative positioning by the director is a deliberate attempt to dismiss the horrific action of sexual violation. The film's use of sentimentality is pervasive in its purported leveling of everybody as equally racist or prejudiced, but is this really what the film does? We are allowed to have empathy for the police officer Ryan, to understand his "pain" and pent-up frustration, through not only verbal storytelling but also scene after scene of his interactions with his father and coworkers. The director is banking on the ambivalence of the audience to not necessarily condone but understand and find some empathy for Ryan's sexual violation toward another black woman, who speaks up in protest.

Therefore, Ryan's character unfolds as a part of a hierarchy of character development.

bell

While we go to films and see more people of color than ever before, we are still watching the same hierarchy of character development and placement. We are allowed to have greater empathy for the Ryan character because empathy is based on awareness and understanding, and we are allowed to understand him more.

Gilda

The power of the state is ubiquitous in this film. The Don Cheadle character is a plain clothes detective who stands in contrast to other male characters.

bell

While we see his rage and hostility, we don't really see the basis for his feelings. We don't know about his father. We see the contempt he shows for his mother as well as his yearning for her regard. In spite of these conflicting emotions, we don't really see anything about the development of his character. We don't see him show any genuine empathy toward other people.

Gilda

This one-dimensional character construction in Hollywood films has been a trait of director Haggis's early work as a writer of the successful TV series *Walker: Texas Ranger,* starring Chuck Norris, who week after week displayed his martial arts against villains. Haggis's more recent work is as scriptwriter for the film *Million Dollar Baby,* where we learn about every character's life beyond the boxing ring. Even the mentally challenged male character, who we briefly view in the film, has a back story outside his connection to boxing. However, we learn nothing of the Morgan Freeman character beyond his failed attempt and physical tragedy within the world of boxing.

With the Don Cheadle character in *Crash,* yes, we do meet his mother. As we enter her home she is introduced by a slow pan of lovely contemporary family James Van Der Zee's black-and-white photographs of African American couples smiling, black children in sports activities, and men in military uniforms and suits. However, at the end of this pan, there is drug paraphernalia on the table. So there you have it, a good family, yet the black woman will be a drug-addicted crazed mother who even in her drugged stupor blames her "successful" son for her misery. She is both heroine mama and Sapphire in one. Haggis expanded the stereotypical roles to make them dynamic in that the people of color are not just one stereotype but can embody two at the same time. Such a device leaves the audience with—well, she came from an intact family, however, due to personal weaknesses or total lack of agency, the black family "reduces" itself to single women heads of households. And these single black woman heads of households are a "tangle of pathology" which reaffirms the 1965 racist and sexist statements the deceased Senator Daniel Moynihan made to discredit black women and blame them for the problems of the black family, therefore rendering invisible the growing feminization of poverty, as well as keeping hidden the injuries of the interlocking oppression of race, class, gender. Such interlocking oppressions in these post–Hurricane Katrina and post–9/11 times have wreaked havoc with women globally and in our local communities. The offense against black women is particularly overt, and Haggis does this demonstratively through his male characters.

bell

Here again we have the image of the black mother in this film which parallels that of the mother in the film *Antwone Fisher.* Both films portray the black mother in a degraded, dehumanized state. She is monstrous. This is the image of black womanhood that mainstream culture exploits right now.

The bodies of black women become the field in which the white pornographic patriarchal fantasies are enacted. They become the weapons white male dominators use against black masculinity. In this white male fantasy of black womanhood, the black female is toxic poison to everyone she comes in contact with, irrespective of color, class, education, or caste. The ultimate message of *Crash* is that blackness is death. And it is only by eliminating blackness that white supremacy can survive and thrive.

In *Crash,* black people have no fathers. Yet there are great white fathers on all levels of the film. There are public white male fathers who are political leaders. Then there are private white fathers who are aging, vulnerable, and worthy of our regard. When we enter the private zone of the elder white man, the fascist state police character Ryan, his caring son, is humanized. The message is conveyed that the white male "father" may be a pseudo-Hitler out in the public world but in private life he is compassionate and caring. We don't see any black person in the film showing compassion and caring for an elder.

Gilda

No compassion for an elder nor compassion or caring for black women. This is particularly true in the representations of the two young black men in *Crash,* the Ludacris and Larenz Tate characters, who are introduced having a diatribe on "racial discrimination" that seems interesting at first, but just as the pan of photographs in the home of the Don Cheadle character's mother begins with possibility, Haggis's script ambushes any glimpse of systemic analysis from young black urban males. Their discussions of racism or disenfranchisement are redirected time and time again. Initially, these two characters indict black women as the purveyors of black male stereotypes. Ludacris's character comments "don't black women think in stereotypes?" and goes on to say "when is the time you ever met a black woman who didn't think she knew everything about your lazy ass?" Once again, black women are the culprits.

bell

One sure comment anyone can make about *Crash* is that it definitely gets the award for depicting the most hateful representations of black masculinity we have seen in a film for a very long time. That's particularly ironic given the fact that this film has many more black characters than most Hollywood films, and that these representations would appear when political pundits and policy makers are telling the public how deeply disenfranchised black males are. *Crash* puts forth the conservative viewpoint which says black males are choosing their own disenfranchisement. It is almost as though *Crash* is the conservative representation of Orlando Patterson's view that black people are suffering not because of oppression and poverty but because of their cultural values. And it is no accident that the repository of blackness and cultural values lies with the two young males who are portrayed as pseudo–gangsta rappers, hip-hop fans. This fictive urban construction of blackness, of black identity, is an east coast transplant taken from the east coast ghetto scene and put in the California landscape. That's partially what makes it melodramatic and strange in that landscape.

Haggis's film suggests all black people are insane and black males are particularly insane. If sanity is that we can face reality, then insanity is that we live in a world of fantasy. What we really see in this film is youthful black masculinity trapped in a doomed world of fantasy— it can't survive. That world is experienced by the younger son with the Saint Christopher medal. Even with Christianity, his spirituality is outside the context of traditional black spiritual culture. It can't sustain him, it can't redeem him. It cannot even link him to anybody else. When he attempts to use his spiritual totem to connect with the younger white cop, he is betrayed. Since this meeting is a symbolic homosocial/homoerotic encounter, the film suggests white gay males are to blame for the genocide black males face.

Gilda

He dies at the hands of the "liberal."

bell

Yes! The film tells naïve black people they should not seek to connect with white liberals for it is only the conservative world that can offer the hope of salvation. The homophobic subtext reinforces the notion that only a fierce hetero-patriarchal regime can save blackness.

People have said that this film is so wonderful because it is realistic. This is totally not a realistic portrait of black culture. Even when we talk about these war zones that many black communities have become, it is the elders in those communities who in fact weave a tapestry of whatever stability there is. Of course, in Haggis's black world, the construction of blackness made by an unenlightened white male, there are no black elders. White men who make Hollywood films have never been interested in our black elders.

Think about the idea of blackness that captures the white pornographic imagination. In this film it is the imagination of the young black buck, the sexualized black man. Don Cheadle's character offers viewers yet another version of a "sweet sweetback," a perverse world of sexual predation. He is the hyper-sexualized male who sees women as either Madonna or whore. He has the idealized mother who degrades herself, yet he feels bound to her. He can't degrade her because she is already degraded by the circumstance of her addiction. He degrades the other women in his life. Once again, we have the black male represented as the harshest, most brutal misogynist.

When people talk about *Crash,* they don't question a white male representation of black men in such a violating and violent way. They accept these images as an accurate portrayal of who black men are.

Gilda

As James Baldwin says, "The Negro performer is still in battle with the white man's image of the Negro—which the white man clings to in order not to be forced to revise the image of himself."

bell

Rage and contempt are the emotions all the black male characters in *Crash* share irrespective of their class. This dehumanizing contempt is glamorized by filmmakers. Usually when I write a critical essay about a film, I watch it 10 to 20 times. I chose not to write an essay about *Crash* because the images of black people are so negative, so degrading, I did not want those images in my head. I did not want to be turning them over in my mind.

There is nothing radical or interventionist about these images. As stated before, they are the same old stereotypical images of blackness offered by the racialized pornographic white imagination. *Crash* has the same clichéd melodramatic elements of *Gone with the Wind* and Douglas Sirk's *Imitation of Life*. We can go down the line from *Birth of a Nation* to see this sort of construction of the raging darkie, the black buck in heat. Only the white males are able to transcend their rage. They are reinscribed as the epitome of the civilized mind. The film tells viewers they may be fascist but they are able to move beyond narrow constructions of identity to save others.

Gilda

It is as if racism and white supremacy are natural, and therefore any attempts to dismantle them are ineffective, so we must use tolerance.

However, as journalism professor Robert Jensen and documentary film producer Robert Wosnitzer write in *Znet,* the film *Crash* promotes "faux humanism and a simplistic message of tolerance [which] directs attention away from a white supremacist system and undermines white accountability for the maintenance of that system."

bell

Sadly, *Crash* is a film folks are using to engage in a public discourse about race. It seems on the surface to be transgressive just by openly talking about race and racism, but ultimately it's a conservative discourse the public hears from the conservative right. The message is that racism is not real—prejudice is real and everyone has these feelings or that it is natural for people who differ based on race or nationality to be in conflict. All of these conservative messages are reinscribed in the film *Crash.*

Crash is interesting to many viewers because we rarely get racialized narratives where there are all kinds of people of color. In a consumer capitalist market that is willing to exploit issues of race and identity, *Crash* has something for everyone. It brings in the Middle East, it brings in Hispanic and Asian cultures. Like the Benetton ads tagline "we are the world," it exploits the notion of diversity. However, the message is we are the conservative world, and because we all hold these imperialist white supremacist capitalist patriarchal views, there can be no accountability. If everyone is racist, then who can be accountable for racism?

Note that in this cinematic world of diverse images the image of the calm obedient Hispanic man contrasts with the image of the raging, contemptuous, evil black man. Here, you have the idealized dehumanized image of Hispanic male as calmer and gentler, embodying a white supremacist vision of the perfect "colored" citizen.

This film has a commentary on citizenship. It is dealing with the question of who is a real American. And it uses the body of the

Hispanic man to say the kind of person of color that mainstream culture wants to be a citizen is someone that, no matter how he is abused, will turn the other cheek. Even when it comes to the potential murder of his daughter, he will not express rage—he will not fight back. In *Crash,* there is this hyper-fixation on black rage that is practically pornographic, and at the same time the film says nothing productive can come out of this black rage. The ideal citizen is, in fact, the citizen who turns the other cheek, who does not critique, who does not dissent or transgress in any way. These men of color who resist can never be citizens. Consider the hostility white supremacist nationalism turned on Spanish-speaking people when they were saying they can both be in this country and identified with their homeland. This film silences that discourse and replaces it with a passive discourse that says all Hispanics are to be hard-working citizens. The Hispanic voice says we want to be your slaves and servants. The message of the Hispanic man imparts that he just wants to do his job and go home to his family.

Gilda

This is reinforced again and again in *Crash* through the stereotype of Miss Anne found in the upper-middle-class wife of the district attorney played by Sandra Bullock. She makes racist comments toward every person of color in the film, then suddenly experiences a pseudo-redemption as one of her final actions in the film. After a fall down the stairs, she embraces her Hispanic maid and says, "You're my best friend." There is not even the slightest bit of chagrin or even facial mortification from the Hispanic maid, thus reinscribing once again the kind of character we expect for the model minority. Just take abuse because the white woman racist will turn into the benevolent dictator à la Miss Anne, and she will embrace you in the end.

The male Asian representation in this film is depicted as a mafia gangster ready to enslave other Asians and is accompanied by his "dragon lady" wife who will do his bidding. And the mistakenly "Arab" Persian store owner is given the familiar stereotype of terrorist who is ready to kill other people of color. This is staged ridiculously as he waits outside the "contented" Hispanic character's home while watching his victim's little daughter come home from school, greeted in her idyllic neighborhood by her loving mother, whose lines in the film are mostly screams. The camera places a medium close-up on the Persian character watching this idyllic scene with his gun in tow, as he patiently waits to kill the father in this working-class Hispanic version of an Ozzie and Harriet family. These representations support the United States' recent fascist policies on immigration. Such notions drive a wedge in the solidarity between and among immigrant populations and domestic people of color.

bell

Overall, this film has an extraordinarily conservative message on race. But it is even more conservative about class and gender. In every situation in this film, women are subordinated. It is as though the feminist movement never happened. The misogynist exchange of women's bodies is akin to what Gayle Rubin describes in her groundbreaking essay "The Traffic in Women." *Crash* begins with a focus on sexuality and gender. Here you have the sense of the fantasy of the upper class: that in the upper class we have this freaky sexuality that the pseudo-rich black man (although the film never makes it clear how rich he is) is the symbolic "rapist" wanting his wife to suck his dick in his vehicle.

This scenario is reminiscent of the real-life Hugh Grant spectacle when he was caught with a gorgeous black woman prostitute sucking his dick. This is no new image of black womanhood. It is the same old racialized and sexualized image. The new twist is the message that no matter what class a black woman is, scratch her and she is still a ho. She will be this vulgar disgusting figure. When the Don Cheadle character shows contempt for the gorgeous Hispanic woman he is sexually using, she is passive. She does not speak to him with hatred nor does she belittle him. When she seeks to connect with his mother, he mocks her. He mocks any idea of solidarity between women. Women, in his eyes, are merely competitors with one another. Hispanic, white, and black women are all fighting for male attention in this patriarchal hierarchy.

Gilda

In fact, the film opens with the language of racial stereotypes being traded between the Latina women and the Korean women characters mocking each other's accents and throwing back and forth the racist stereotypes we all learn from white supremacy. And finally the film ends with the Shiniqua character expressing similar notions of racial stereotypes that were said to her by the Ryan character: "What the hell is wrong with you people....Don't even speak to me unless you speak American." However, these incidents are never placed within their origins of white supremacist capitalist patriarchy. They are positioned in the narrative to support the idea that prejudice and racism is innate in all of us, part of everyday discourse, and arises naturally in certain contexts.

Even the black woman political figure played by Nona Gaye, who is the symbolic Condoleezza Rice in the film, competes with other women. She is the passive shadow self of the white wife of the district attorney.

bell

It is this silent pact between the white male district attorney and the black woman Nona Gaye character that we contrast with the historical figure of white women, Miss Anne, wife of the district attorney. Yet it is the public alliance between white male power and his subordinates that lets viewers know where the real power lies on the political scene: shared allegiance to do whatever is needed to maintain power.

Gilda

The relationship between power and race is honestly portrayed in David Cronenberg's film *A History of Violence,* in which even when the sweet middle-class white family finds out that the mild-mannered father was a hit man of sorts there is a brief break and then a silent pact to maintain their secret about his ever present past. He rejoins them at the proverbial dinner table, and they, with blond hair and compliance in silence, break bread together, eating bland food.

bell

A History of Violence is a remarkable film. It brilliantly exposes how patriarchy, that dominator culture, requires violence to sustain itself. As a family, they agree to be silent about their shared allegiance to using violence to maintain control. The black woman "shadow wife" who stands by her white man and his family mimics Condoleezza Rice's adoration of Bush and allegiance to his imperialistic regime of white power. Any black woman who repudiates this unholy alliance cannot survive. Depicted as a willing accomplice to her own degradation, she can have no redemptive sexuality.

Gilda

In *Crash,* Haggis gives us a glimpse of this pseudo-secret sexualized relationship between the two. But of course, the Nona Gaye character never gets to live this out; on camera, she stays in the background with little to offer in scripted lines or close-ups. She is symbolically seen in mostly long shots down gilded hallways of federal buildings or with a non-expressive gaze when in medium close-ups, particularly when she is overtly dismissed whenever any decisions are to be made. The lights go down on her and she disappears.

bell

As a sexualized metaphor, the lighting choice renders her an object of desire, just as the film starts with the image of the Thandie Newton character going down on her husband. Women in this film are all falling down-subjugated-re-subordinated.

Gilda

To contrast the reactions of the black middle-class husband and the white district attorney, we still see more care and concern for the wife coming from the district attorney. When the Newton character comes to her husband's job to make amends the night after her sexual violation, and their subsequent argument, her husband, the Terrence Howard character, tells her to go home and gestures for her to shut up when he does not want to hear her voice.

bell

The black male's brutal contempt and dismissal of his wife contrasts with that of the caring white man who holds her in his arms. The message viewers get is that no matter how brutal males in authority are in the public eye, they maintain a tender and caring side. In contrast, black males are beasts. Truly, if black men were at all organized in this nation, they would be standing up and saying that they are not as this movie *Crash* portrays them.

And remember that the Cronenberg film *A History of Violence* is an incredible deconstruction of whiteness and the dehumanization of the sexualized white body. Haggis's film is a shallow cloned use of this image. The narrative of sexuality in *Crash* is continually racialized. Focusing on race, people avoid looking at the raw moments of patriarchal pornographic sexuality in the film where women are being re-subjugated again and again. Gender misogynist warfare is enacted on the bodies of "colored" women. White women are protected and safe. Then there is the homophobia in this film, evoked by the crass racial bonding between two young men: the young white liberal cop Hansen and the young black male played by Larenz Tate. Hansen is portrayed as someone ruled by both desire and fear. He picks up the young black male in a scene of symbolic cruising, yet his fear leads him to murder the blackness he desires. This homophobic construct of the symbolic gay white male as killer, as monster, underscores one of the conservative messages of *Crash:* don't think you can trust a liberal white person. They will be the first to destroy black people. Put your trust in white fascists, they will save you and jump over their hatred and contempt in order to be heroic.

Gilda

So, once again, *Crash* falls into the classic Hollywood mode, only this time the black person does not die in the first five minutes of the film but in the last five minutes or so of the film. But, rest assured, there is usually this kind of narrative tagging whenever there are black people in a Hollywood film.

bell

Of course, there is nothing in the history of fascist whiteness that suggests whiteness ever forgets itself and surrenders its power to rescue colonized blackness. That's why this film is so profoundly dishonest.

In *Crash,* the bodies of black people are exploited by white power. It's just another plantation culture. That this film is one that will be used as a way to have a provocative discussion about race is ironic given that it is really the sexuality that so captivates audiences and the interplay of conflict between white and black bodies. The ingredients that make Hollywood Hollywood—sex, violence, violation, and action—are all present in *Crash*. One of the reasons audiences don't want to see Spike Lee's *Four Little Girls* as a way to engage public discourse about race is because this film offers no sentimentalized portrait of white power, it is shown as damaging to everyone. *Four Little Girls* shows that there is a system of domination that is maintained by certain hierarchies of power. This system wounds everyone. *Four Little Girls* is such a compelling film because we are allowed to see how white supremacy and racist exploitation and oppression hurt everyone. Black people in this film have integrity and love and show no contempt toward our enemy. We don't see that in *Crash* because everybody is seen as an agent of pain. There are innocent people in *Four Little Girls*. The little girls are innocent. Their families that never recovered were not to blame for this racist slaughter. No film has exposed the post-traumatic stress caused by racism as Lee's documentary. It's tragic if people will not see a fine film like *Four Little Girls,* which is an unsentimental realistic examination of race and racism in our nation. Even though *Crash* is a fiction film, it is shot as though it is a documentary. That is part of its seductive appeal.

But Haggis is not an excellent filmmaker. He appropriates scenes from the films *Pulp Fiction, Do the Right Thing,* Robert Altman's *Short Cuts,* and other such films with multiple narratives. The guys in the restaurant could be a complete cloning of Spike Lee's moment in *Do the Right Thing.* Perhaps this is why the film has such an appeal. It took so much from other films; it is a clichéd and, sadly, all-too-familiar narrative.

Unlike *Four Little Girls,* which shares the powerful concept that we are all disturbed by racism, *Crash* suggests that racism is "natural"— that everyone is racist. Hence, it denies the reality of racism. While everyone is capable of prejudice, everyone does not have the power to exploit and oppress others. Rather than offering us a message that could bring deeper understanding, *Crash* keeps us stuck in a racist quagmire—the only ones who escape are the white heroes. White power prevails in *Crash.*

10

A Pornography of Violence: A Dialogue About *Precious*

bell hooks with filmmaker Gilda L. Sheppard

Writing critical essays on film was once vital to me as a cultural critic because I observed that by viewing movies diverse individuals of all races, classes, and genders could and would engage critical thinking. When folks saw a film, especially one that stimulated their imagination, I found them eager to talk about it, eager to share what they liked and disliked. As a feminist thinker I was especially interested in engaging issues of gender. Fundamentally, I knew that films do not just show us the culture we live in as it is but that they also create culture. And that's what I wanted to call attention to: what were films creating when they highlighted issues of race, class, and gender.

In those heady days I usually would write about a film if it excited my imagination, if it stirred me emotionally. One of the most exciting essays about film that I have written was the one on Quentin Tarantino's film *Pulp Fiction*. I was living in New York City at the time during a harsh winter and seeing the film was like getting blood transfusion. I could feel the intensity of my response to the movie in every part of my pent-up being and body. Coming home to my fifth floor walk-up in the West Village, I was eager to document my thoughts about this film. To say that I was over-stimulated would be putting it mildly. When I reached the top floor I found the heat had gone off once again (only in New York City!) and the place was freezing. Unaccustomed to working on the computer, I sat down on the red chair and tried to write with hat, coat, and gloves on. I felt truly desperate to release all the passions the film had stirred in me. Ultimately, I had to take the gloves off and work at the computer, with hands cold and still. I sat there for hours writing until everything the film had stirred up inside me was released, let go. And there it was all ready for me to find someone to read all that I had written.

Few films have excited as much passion. Certainly, Spike Lee's work stirs me. And because I write strong critiques of his films, readers think I do not like his work. They misunderstand. Spike Lee's *Four Little Girls* is an excellent film, one that moved me heart and soul. Every citizen of this nation should see it. For me, insightful critique exists in a world beyond like and dislike; it is all about passionate response, whether positive or negative. Rarely, do I see a film that has no redeeming value. Readers have responded positively to my work on films. Essays on movies are the most re-printed and taught of my work. I stopped writing about film because I felt that I reached a point where I was looking at work from the perspective of feminist thinking about race, gender, and class and more often than not I was not seeing anything that was saying anything new. Most of the films I watched were just disappointing.

Filmmaker and critic Gilda L. Sheppard, who teaches my work with as much passion as I write, encouraged me to write about the film *Precious*. I was not moved to write; the film simply was not compelling. Let's face it: *Precious* was just another in a long line of really bad movies. However, Gilda did persuade me to talk with her about the film. Here are remnants of our conversation:

bell

We are living in the past—living and reproducing what I call plantation culture. It is no new phenomenon. Plantation culture is what happens in colonization when one colonizing force takes over, finds aspects of the culture that they—the colonizers—have been actively destroying, and decide "let's keep these 'artifacts' and bring them back to sell to the folk from whom they were originally stolen"—selling it back to them in a cruel and bastardized and even rotten form. Think of it like food. Enslaved Africans working in agriculture grew all these wonderful organic vegetables but what the masters gave them to eat was the rotten stuff—the slop. Ironically, today black folks with class privilege can produce the slop and sell it back to us; if we so choose we too can be colonizers. *Precious* exemplifies this plantation culture—its makers and marketers have been black folks.

This film reminded me of the historical marketing of the Hottentot Venus, where a black female body that did not fit the norm was displayed for the prurient pornographic gaze of white folks. Only in this case this film is packaged as though it has social significance; the public is told that it's a film that will confront viewers with the tragedy of incest, that audiences must be prepared before they watch. Like a labeled poison: just be prepared before you take it. In this film we basically see a very dark-skinned obese black female teenager who is, according to the aesthetics of white supremacy, not only ugly, she is monstrous. There are many beautiful young black females who are obese but this young woman was chosen because she could be made to appear as the complete opposite of beauty. In the fairy-tale tradition she is the beast. Black folk have been on display (the slave auction block) in cages throughout our history. And especially the dark black female body, which embodies that which is most hated in white supremacist culture.

Gilda

Obesity, incest, domestic violence, living in a crack-infested community, physical and sexual child abuse in the home is the constant repetitive subject matter of this film. The entire community where Precious lives—the neighbors in the apartment buildings—all are mothers and children who show no love or resistance, only compliance with the perpetuation of criminality as if there is no movement for social change in poor neighborhoods. No wonder justice is practiced as punishment. These are intergenerational criminals with no redeeming qualities.

bell

Since media tells us constantly that poverty is ugly, monstrous, how can there be redeeming qualities?

Gilda

In his work *Yo' Mama's Disfunktional!*, black historian Robin Kelley reminds us that when it comes to the black poor, "Our dysfunctionality fascinates; it is alluring." This allure attracted former First Lady Barbara Bush enough to organize a special showing of *Precious* for her friends. Explaining her actions, Bush noted: "I think it stereotyped Precious as a black. This could have been anybody, anyplace in

America. Sad to say, children are abused. It could have been white, brown, yellow, whatever—whatever. And I hate that because it isn't just blacks, it's everybody....It is an American problem."

bell

Yet Bush had not had showings of inspired films that look at the issue of child abuse in all its manifestation. And like so many Americans, she apparently cannot understand the fact that incest is not an issue of poverty, but that it reaches across class and race. Yet she equates this "American problem" with black folks.

Gilda

Let's look at how America deals with problems. The United States has the largest incarcerated population in the world, and as legal scholar Michelle Alexander writes, more African Americans today are in prison, on parole, or on probation than were enslaved in 1859. Women comprise nearly seven percent of the U.S. prison population. Yet there is no legal attempt to punish the mother and father of Precious, for all the abuse she suffers, including incest....I am reminded of the comment by James Baldwin about the destruction of black life: "They...do not know it and do not want to know it. It is the innocence which constitutes the crime." This is the master narrative in this film whether it is intentional or not. Like everything else in our society, the film depicts brutal injustice while simultaneously condoning it. You state this in the book *Reel to Real* when you contend: "Whether you like it or not, cinema assumes a pedagogical role in the lives of many people. It may not be the intent of a filmmaker to teach audiences anything, but that does not mean that lessons are not learned." Certainly, there was something that compelled me and my students to see the film. One of the seventeen-year-old girls felt that she was "forced to look."

And what many folks felt forced to look at was what in their minds was the epitome of ugliness both as expressed in the monstrous body of Precious and the monstrous ugliness of the abuse afflicted on her. I am not one of those folks who believe that black people should hide the dehumanizing aspects of our lives. We know incest happens every day in black communities, just as it happens in all communities in our nation. And it is all about abuse whether the victim is beautiful and privileged. It is no less painful, no less dehumanizing, no less tragic. The story of Precious that the film tells is really a horror story—a world of unrelenting everyday abuse and intimate terrorism. It was presented as a narrative of autobiographical confession; however, in my writing on confession I emphasize that it is not enough to simply tell our story. Telling a personal story in and of itself is not profound; it's what we make of that story. And *Precious* has no story beyond the tragedy of incest. And she is not even allowed a space in the film to tell this story. Her story is a small secret tale of addiction to fantasy. We learn nothing deep about Precious; she is the silent victim. The person in the film who has a story, who tells her story in a manner that leads audiences to empathize with her pain, is the mother. She is never silent. And her story is a tale of abuse and abandonment. When she sits in a face-to-face confrontation with the social worker and speaks of the lovelessness of her life, demanding to know "who is going to love me," her pain is made visible. Precious never engages in acts of existential self-reflection. She cannot articulate her trauma. The mother really provides a story of trauma, one that is ongoing, passed down from generation to generation. So the film poses the question "who will love the black body"; and it gives us the answer: "no one." And in place of healthy self-esteem and love black folks will be given fantasy. And surprise, surprise almost every fantasy Precious reveals is about whiteness, about longing to be white. Although this movie was supposedly a film version of the book *Push*, all the white characters that appear in the film make up the characters of every fantasy. So the film offers a pedagogy of self-hatred, telling viewers again and again that black folks worship whiteness, that if we could only be white, have the beauty of whiteness, we would be saved, we would not be victims of abusive trauma. Such fantasies are dehumanizing as they negate the reality of abuse in the lives of real people, black and white, irrespective of class. This film so fixated on the worship of whiteness that it was frightening. Ironically, the liberating treasure that makes success possible in the world of western civilization that is valorized in Sapphire's novel is education, specifically literacy. But literacy is never the subject of fantasy for Precious in the film version. She does not dream of being a teacher. Her fantasy is that she is a celebrity, worshipped by the crowd. A celebrity to whom we bring love. Literacy and the struggle to be truly literate is not an issue in the film. Like incest it is a tale told in the background. The narrative that is at the center of the film is the worship of whiteness. And it is this worship that violates and assaults Precious and all the black children like her.

Gilda

Included in this fantasy is the praise of capitalism. Of course this fantasy is expressed in both subtle and blatant ways as "the American Dream" and also as a worship of whiteness in black face, almost minstrelsy but masked by the notion of liberation and redemption. I remember you were writing about Stan Brakhage's work and quoting him stating, about film, that: "All this slavish mirroring of the human condition feels like a bird singing in front of mirrors....Film must be free from all imitations, of which the most dangerous is the imitation of life."

bell

Again and again I emphasize in my work and art practices that "art does not exist to simply mirror reality." If this were the case, there would be no need for art. Yet, when I raised critical questions about *Precious* to black audiences, I was told that the film is "real and raw," that it is "telling it like it is." In actuality, it not real—the filmic narrative is an interpretation of a fantasy projected onto real black people. *Push* is a novel. The author has stated in interviews that she constructed the character of Precious from a composite of black students she encountered working as a substitute teacher. Yet the character Precious in the film is presented as an example of the fate of any black child in a poor black community. In her important work *Killing the Black Body*, Dorothy Roberts explains that one form the attack on poor black families takes in imperialist white supremacist capitalist patriarchy is the insistence that poor and underclass black folk are always at risk of being dehumanized and that children in such families would fare better if they were taken away from their families. And Roberts emphasizes that in many cases it is white people who want black children pushing the idea that all poor and underclass black families are unfit. One aspect of the film *Precious* that was particularly annoying was the construction of the grandmother as passively accepting the vicious abuse of her grandchild. When the mother is not beating Precious or shaming her, what the grandmother does is to render her invisible—the ultimate objectification. Yet folks say this is "real." The real truth is that black grandmothers do the work of functional parenting in black families of all classes. Yet they are also depicted as ugly and monstrous in this film, complicit in the dehumanization of Precious. And through it all, viewers of the film are told that we should empathize with her pain—but the scenes in the film do not invite empathy or critical reflection about her plight. Instead the audiences are subjected to flashbacks of the father raping her. The father is absent. He has no voice, no name, no identity. He is simply depicted as a good-looking buck who is also a violent sexual predator. These scenes are reminiscent of the sex scenes in the film *Sweet Sweetback*. Audiences for the film are stimulated and entertained by the violence they watch perpetuated by both the mother and the father. Sadly the horrific abuse we see in the film does not mirror the everyday predatory

violence inflicted on children by adults. More often than not children
are abused by folk they know, folk who show them kindness. Toni
Morrison explored this in her first novel, *The Bluest Eye*. As I stated
when we began, many folks wanted me to write about the film *Precious* but what is more interesting than this terribly bad film is the
emotional need of audiences in our culture who want to consume this
sentimental slop and act like it is documentary investigative journalism
announcing itself with headlines like "today we are turning the spotlight on incest in black communities." And yet there is no meaningful
exploration of incest. Even when Precious is given care by teachers
and the social worker, no one directly addresses sexual abuse and how
she might heal from it. Indeed, the best the film can do is suggest
that learning to read is a viable substitute for receiving the therapy
that would help one have the courage to heal. Simply depicted violent
abuse is not redemptive. If life is truly as ugly and horrific as this film
suggests, if it's all ugly shit, then we do not need art to give us more
shit. Art should and can be the place where we are given an alternative,
a redemptive vision. The book *Push* was a very short melodramatic
narrative which does not have the embellished glamorous world of
fantasy depicted in the film. It offers a vision of literacy that is connected to critical reflection as a place of redemption and hope. The
film addresses education as the practice of freedom as a sub-textual
narrative when it is central in the book.

Gilda

Yes, it was these scenes in the classroom at the "alternative school"
Each One Teach One where we are forced to look at Precious and
possibly confront why we view her as ugly, angry, and dumb and
freeze this frame not as a Hollywood stereotype but as the politics of
our looking relations. Consider the way the diverse young women
introduce themselves by sharing details of their life: we see them in the
act of creating a learning community then moving from the metaphor

of what is your favorite color to what is it you do well. In this effort to create a learning community, despite their differences, there is a sense of agency and imagination of possibility—as Toni Morrison says in "The Sight of Memory," imagining for the "purpose of the work becoming." These scenes are not talked about when the film is praised or critiqued. Sisterhood is an expression and active form of bonding within the urban ghetto. Yet the film never moves past the feel-good question to explore the deeper critical issues of PTSD, incest, patriarchy, young single motherhood, poverty, love, and fear. Precious attempts to make an analysis of political economy when she considers her options of workforce/welfare at school. She sees the inequity yet it does not serve as a meaningful catalyst for individual social change. After this quick scene the film moves to a narrative jump cut without using this opportunity to link theory and practice, with coming to critical consciousness and creating concrete changes. Instead we get the hallmark card message of "it is ok—you can make it!" This feel-good-about-yourself tone is set at the beginning of the film when we see in the background a strange graffiti print which says "everything is a gift of the universe." Yet in the universe in which Precious lives negative messages abound, and the face of survival is one of anger and resentment. I remember E-40's line "I got a mirror in my pocket and I practice looking hard." The look of anger is so present among youth in urban America and it is the look on Precious's face throughout most of film until she attends the alternative school. There, at last, Precious finds her voice. These scenes are not talked about because they are not melodramatic; they do not have the dramatic appeal of violence. The classroom scenes in the "alternative" school demonstrate literacy as social justice, as agency, as an ability to cultivate the oppositional gaze.

bell

But these scenes are consumed by melodrama, much as Precious is consumed by the abusive violence in the film. We get the colonial image of Precious cooking food as a "plantation culture" image that lingers. White folks get offered a film like *Julie and Julia* (another female coming-of-age in the city) and black folks get Precious running with stolen fried chicken and eating hairy ham hocks; they get love and we get heart attacks. Strange, isn't it, that a few folks involved in the making and promotion of this film have been the victims of verbal, physical, and sexually violent abuse as children. Simply being the victim of abuse does not mean that anyone has a clear understanding of the healing process. Most folks are driven by sentimentality, like Oprah. There is no doubt in my mind that she sincerely cares about black children who are abused. Yet that does not change the reality that this film is a capitalist production that aims to bring in the big bucks and the big fame. Tyler Perry, Oprah, Lee Daniels—they are all about the success of this money-making project. And that agenda is more primary than creating greater cultural awareness of the trauma of incest. Just because one is black and makes art about black people, does not mean that the art is about justice and therefore requires of viewers a capacity to look at the political ramifications of a work of art. We have very little art produced by anybody of any color that has justice or democracy as a central theme of any idea of freedom and liberation. Certainly, I am not saying that we are meant to be prescriptive and that art should only be about justice. Rather, I'm arguing that art can be aesthetically interesting and politically progressive. There is very little art of the Hollywood variety that is directed toward raising consciousness and engaging excellent aesthetics. Artworks that make use of the tropes of plantation culture (i.e., the imperialist white supremacist capitalist patriarchal paradigms) maintain the status quo. Many working-class black folks who saw *Precious* thought the film was full of stereotypical exaggerated entertaining violence; it was primarily folks with class privilege who saw it as an "amazing" film about black poverty, incest, and other ghetto perversions. Precious is abandoned by the film as many poor folk who are the victims of insane violence are abandoned by society. The big scene where Precious is depicted as walking toward a new and better life is nothing but a big lie, a big fantasy.

Gilda

This is the pornography of violence.

bell

Yes. In real life violent, incest rape is happening every day. Children of all classes are violently abused every day by fathers and mothers. The novel *Push* suggested that children could be helped in the healing of trauma by critical literacy, by finding a voice. Certainly, visionary feminist thinkers have continually called attention to the importance of speaking one's story. Yet, the cinematic Precious never acquires a voice or the ability to think critically. Precious and her mother do not undergo therapy together. And the film offers no meaningful positive future of the broken black folk in the film. Without hope the big all-encompassing message of the film is that collectively, poor black folks are doomed. And what is tacitly pushed in the film is that the only black folk who will survive the ongoing holocaust, the genocide perpetuated by plantation culture daily, are the contemporary house servants of imperialist white supremacist capitalist patriarchy. And it is troubling that the bodies of lesbian women are used to push the message of light-skinned class privilege—of bourgeois values. In keeping with the emphasis on fantasy in the film, viewers are encouraged to see this world of hedonistic violence as one where homophobia does not rule the day. In the film every person that is in any way kind to Precious has fair skin and straight hair (in keeping with the insertion of worship of whiteness that the film extols). The black lesbians in the film are hard-drinking, smoking liberals who just want to help. Yet viewers are left to ponder how they can help when their lives seem to be marked by personal "dysfunction." This is the usual way gay life is depicted in cinema—stereotypical and negative. And when negative images of homosexuality are created by homosexuals, it does not make them redemptive. Concurrently, the film does not invite viewers to see fat females, and specifically fat black females, in a new way.

Gilda

And Gabourey Sidibe, the actress who plays the role of Precious chosen for her dark skin and her big body, will probably only play roles where her big body is part of the narrative.

bell

Ultimately, what made the film *Precious* a must-see for many moviegoers was the very pornography of violence that the marketing of the film implied it would critically explore. Viewers of the film are positioned as voyeurs who get a firsthand look into the horrible lives of underclass black folks in an urban ghetto. And it was a fictive raw exposé—no real truths exposed, no real way out for the black folks who are the working slaves on this plantation. That's the hard message of the film; it's all about despair because there is no way out. Comfort your anguish with fantasy because nothing is going to change, nothing will make a difference.

A Community of Caring

Writing about my Kentucky past, I often say little about Rosa Bell (my mother) and Veodis (my father), yet their presence in Kentucky also called me home. Simply put, they were and are getting older, moving closer to death, and I wanted to spend time with them during their process of descent. My father has likened the period of life when one begins to be old as the time when we are no longer walking up the mountain. "Glory," he will say to me, "I'm never going to be walking up the mountain again, I'm going down the mountain. I'm on my way home." His metaphor astounds me because both Rosa and Veodis wanted to turn away from mountains and hills, to turn away from the agrarian life they had been born into, and to seek after the modern and the new. No farming for them, no backbreaking labor on the land. They both wanted life in the city. And, as a child of the country, I have been at odds with them since my birth. Mama, sometimes jokingly and sometimes with rage, would rail against our many differences by exclaiming, "I don't know where I got you from but I sure wish I could take you back!" And oh how much I longed to go back, to go live with my grandparents with whom I felt a greater resonance of spirit. Mama and Daddy would not allow this.

They wanted me to become a city girl, and of all my siblings they wanted me to be the one who would not be "country." And yet in many ways I am as country as they come, more like my grandparents than my parents. I even speak the language of my grandparents, the language of Kentucky black vernacular dialect but I also speak the language of the city, a language that is neutral with no attention to region or place. Hearing me speak the language of city was a comfort to my parents. That is until I acquired a dissident voice, one that shocked and jarred their sensibilities, a voice that made them feel afraid. To them, any speaking out against authority, what I would call dominator culture, puts one at risk. And therefore it is better to remain silent. My talking made them afraid. In some ways they were glad then when I left home and went out into a world of cities where they did not have to hear me talk. They could never grasp that I was just plain country in lots of ways and that no amount of book learning, education, or writerly fame was going to change that.

In *Citizenship Papers,* Wendell Berry boldly states: "I believe that this contest between industrialism and agrarianism now defines the most fundamental human difference, for it divides not just two nearly opposite concepts of agriculture and land use, but also two nearly opposite ways of understanding ourselves, our fellow creatures, and our world." For me, this quote deeply evokes the schism between me and my parents. They represented the city, the culture of the new—make more money, buy more things, throw things away, there is always more. My grandparents, both maternal and paternal, represented the country, the culture of the old, no waste, everything used, useful, recycled. Now Rosa Bell and Veodis have themselves become part of the culture of the old. Dad at eighty-eight is one of the last living survivors of the all-black infantry he was part of in World War II. Mama is ten years younger but the loss of her memory has taken her from here to eternity. She, more so than Dad, feels that she has no real place among the living, that she does not belong. Unlike Dad, she feels it would be better to die.

Losing one's memory to dementia or Alzheimer's is a way of dying. It takes one to a place where you no longer make connections and communicate with the mind. Words no longer carry much weight. Language has little meaning. The divide between the country and the city no longer exists. Time cannot be understood in any consistent linear way. Time converges on itself; days past fall easily into the present, and years collapse upon themselves. Faces, too, fall into forgetfulness and relationships that were once all become indistinct shadows. Mama awakens and says of the husband with whom she has been in partnership for almost sixty years: "Who is he?" When you identify him, she just says, "Oh!" And that is where it ends for her. Later, she will call him by name and speak from that place where they know one another intimately. But this vivid awareness will not last.

Mama still knows who I am. She hears my voice and knows Gloria Jean is calling. She hears my voice and knows how I am feeling. One day I call and she says: "I was just looking at one of your books." When I was home last, she had one of my books and kept reading the part that describes the author. Repeatedly, she reads it aloud to me over and over again. When she finishes, she is satisfied to have grasped a part of who I am—her daughter who writes. And yet my writing has been a source of pain to Mama, revealing to the public world much that she would have chosen to keep private, to keep secret. Even though she told me once that my work causes her so much pain that she just has to fall on her knees and pray, she is proud of my writing. Both my parents have weathered the storm of my work. Dysfunctional though our family may be, they have maintained their care and commitment to all their children—to family. And, as I have grown into mid-life, I have come to appreciate deeply the discipline it takes to maintain commitment for more than fifty years. Living alone as I have done for almost as many years of my life as I shared with a partner, seeing marriages, partnerships (straight and gay) come and go, falling apart at the slightest moment where difference is recognized and deemed irreconcilable, I appreciate the strength it takes to maintain commitment.

I appreciate and understand a vision of marriage as a sacrament. P. Travis Kroeker gives beautiful expression to what this means when he shares from a Christian standpoint that "giving ourselves away in marriage is an occasion of joy—we celebrate it because as humans we are made for intimate communion with God and with all of life." Explaining further, he contends: "The sacrament of marriage is therefore anything but a private, exclusive act. It is always related to the larger community of which it is a part. One of the greater dangers of romantic love is that it privatizes love, depriving it of essential nutrients. A flourishing marriage needs the community to sustain it and will in turn build up the community and the life of the world." Indeed, I see this made evident in my parents' long marriage and saw it in the marriage of more than seventy years of my maternal grandparents. Sadly, both these marriages were not particularly loving or joyful. Even so, the conditions for love were present—care, commitment, knowledge, responsibility, respect, and trust. All parties involved simply chose not to honor them in their wholeness. They chose instead to focus on care and commitment. As a witness to their lives, I can testify that they were fine disciplined examples of these two aspects of love. And despite the lack of sustained well-being in their marriages, I am still awed and impressed by the power of their will to commit. I long for such lifelong commitment in the context of a loving relationship.

Significantly, these two marriages lasted so long precisely because they took place in the context of community. They were buttressed by the constant interplay of life within extended family, church, work, and a civic world—a life in community. When I began to move past my harsh critiques of my parent's marriage, of their dysfunction, I could see positive aspects of their bonding. I could even feel envy.

What I most admired and admire about their life is their capacity for disciplined commitment, their engagement in making and sustaining a life in community. And even though they did not create for themselves a loving bond, they did prepare the ground for love by sowing two important seeds—care and commitment—which I take to be essential to any effort to create love. Consequently, I am grateful to them for providing me and my siblings an understanding via their life practice of what sustained commitment and care look like.

I am especially blessed to have lived long enough and to have parents still alive to whom I can express gratitude for their gifts of care and commitment. In his insightful essay, "An Economy of Gratitude," Norman Wirzba shares this understanding: "In the practical, mundane, sustained commitment to place and community the marks of gratitude...come into clearer focus." He defines those marks as "affection, attention, delight, kindness, praise, conviviality, and repentance." All these defining marks are present when I commune with our parents in our native place, in their Kentucky home. Gone is the spirit of conflict and contestation that for years characterized our interactions. By letting us know that there was no conflict that would be powerful enough to shatter ties of care and commitment, our parents, especially our mother, made it possible for there to always be a place of reconciliation, a place to come together, a way to return home.

Wirzba emphasizes the importance of creating a "community of care" so that our relationships with one another can be "governed by conviviality rather than suspicion, by praise rather than blame." Furthermore, he writes: "In a community of care, people are turned toward one another. They have given up the false, perpetually deferred dream that happiness lies somewhere else with other people." That includes embracing our parents, accepting them for being who they are and not for becoming what we wanted or want them to be. Again, Wirzba explains, "As we work with others, and as we endeavor to get to know them, we learn to appreciate them in their depth and integrity and with a better appreciation for their potential and need. We see them for the unique creatures they are and begin to approach the complexity, beauty and mystery of every created thing and person. The loveliness of who they are starts to dawn on us, calling forth within us a response of love and celebration." Certainly, this has been my experience both in my relationship to my parents, the community of my growing up, and now to the place in Kentucky that is my home.

Communities of care are sustained by rituals of regard. Eating together was a central focus of family gatherings in our household. At the table we share our accounts of daily life, humor, and the sheer pleasure of delicious home-cooked food. Our mother was a great cook. I share with Wirzba the belief that "around the table we create the conditions for conviviality and praise....In the sharing of the meal we give concrete expression to our gratitude. We catch a taste of heaven." This was certainly true in the kitchen of our mother's house.

Sadly, in her new state of lost memory, Mama no longer cooks or finds delight in delicious eating. She has to be coaxed to come to the table. This is often the case with those who suffer from dementia or Alzheimer's. New rituals of regard are needed. Before her memory loss, Mama was always on her feet working, cooking, cleaning, meeting someone else's needs. In their patriarchal marriage, she waited on our father hand and foot. Now she needs us to serve her, to dedicate ourselves to her comfort and care. This service is the enactment of a ritual of regard. The devotion she arouses in her loved ones is a natural outcome of the care and commitment she has extended to all of us. And even though it has been hard for Dad to change, to accept the end of certain forms of patriarchal privilege that he has assumed were his birthright simply by having been born male, he is learning to be a caregiver to her.

Nowadays, Mama spends much of her time sitting. There are beautiful and wondrous aspects to her current forms of self-expression and identity. It is a joy to sit next to her, to be able to hold her close, to caress her hands, all gestures that would have been impossible in the past. She would have deemed it silly to be sitting around talking of love when there was work to be done. How wonderful it is to have these new experiences with her converge with the old, to see her so tender, so vulnerable, so without the restraints of shame and conventional inhibitions. Now I see in her the wildness of spirit she once saw in me and wanted to crush for fear it was dangerous. My gratitude that I can be present—a witness to her life now—as she struggles to make sense of the dots that do not connect, as she journeys toward death, knows no bounds. Also it is good to witness Dad gracefully walking down the mountain and giving him now and then a helping hand.

Wirzba believes that "as we dedicate ourselves to one another, and thus experience daily and directly the diverse array of gifts that contribute to our living, gratitude will take its rightful place as the fundamental disposition that guides and forms our ways." Gratitude allows us to receive blessings; it prepares the ground of our being for love. And it is good to see that in the end, when all is said and done—love prevails.

12

Bonding Across Boundaries

Throughout my college years both as a student and a professor, we talked about the positive gifts that come when you bond with someone different from yourself, from a different race, class, gender. It was the grand age of cultural studies. A positive politics of difference was the starting point for forming ties across boundaries, especially those imposed by systems of domination, by imperialist white supremacist capitalist patriarchy. While the theory was all about border crossing, there was little talk about actual practice, of what makes bonding possible across race, class, gender, and diverse politics. Our silence about practice surfaced because no one really wanted to talk about the difficulties of bonding across differences, the breakdowns in communications, the disappointments, the betrayals. While we talked openly about race and gender, not much was stated about the politics of class, even though more often than not it was differences of class that separated and estranged us from one another. Race and gender boundaries seemed easier to surmount than class differences. Yet most of us were raised to believe that class does not matter in a democratic society.

Most of my fellow graduate students have, like me, become teachers. We write and teach feminist theory. We write and teach about race, gender, and sexuality. We write about class. However much of our writing is description and analysis of issues. We write more about theory than we do about practice. It is has simply been easier to do theory than to put into real-life practice what we declare as the work of ending domination, the habits of being that must abound if we are to live in a just society that offers to everyone the right to have a meaningful life of optimal well-being.

Growing up in the state of Kentucky during the years of racial apartheid, I was taught by white and black alike that the races should not mix, that separate but equal was better. While unenlightened racist white folks pushed the notion that the races should be separate because of their innate superiority, black folks advocated separation to keep us safe; to their mind, race mixing usually brought trouble, even death. Daring to cross the boundaries of race in a small town was not easy. Usually it was the religious white folks who cared about justice who made the effort to meet and mix. Individual black folks who mingled with white folks were confronting and challenging the system of imperialist white supremacist domination. We were taking risks. And those risks seemed worth taking if it meant that someday racist apartheid would end. As a teenager hopeful that ending all forms of domination would happen in my lifetime, I was willing to merge the personal and the political, to do my part, however small, to change the world.

It has often amazed me that in today's world—with very little risk involved, no chance of excommunication from one's community and family, no life-threatening attacks—individuals still seem to be terrified of difference, of bonding across boundaries. Even individuals who talk and write about the importance of border crossing still create lives where they are most often interacting with folks like themselves, especially those with whom they share race and class. In my work, in my life, I have found that the primary fear folks have of being with someone unlike themselves is the fear of conflict. And yet, none of us imagine that in our love relationships, with family and kin, that we will never have moments of conflict; it is simply that we believe that in those relationships should conflict arise, we will be able to handle it.

Early on in feminist circles women struggling to bond on the basis of shared sisterhood often found that the point where similarities ended was a breaking-point that led to conflict. And more often than not conflicts became fierce and pulled folks apart. Yet, I would not rejoice in sisterhood across difference as I do today if it were not for my experience working with women who were unraveling white supremacist thought and action from their minds and hearts. With them I witness a genuine politics of solidarity. And even when differences between myself and an individual woman were fierce and at times bitter, commitment to sisterhood brought us back together. One arena of constant conflict happened when white women would ask black women/women of color our thoughts about a decision to be made. And when we would disagree, our comments would be ignored. It was as though we had never spoken.

Those of us creating theories of race and gender saw this as a gesture of white supremacy. Yet what seemed clear to us only became clear to the white females with whom we worked through reading, explanations, and a willingness to do the critical self-examination necessary for taking an objective look at one's behavior. I once had a fierce negative conflict with a women's studies colleague with whom I felt a strong sense of solidarity. I believed her commitment to ending imperialist white supremacist capitalist patriarchy was as firm as my own. Yet repeatedly she would ignore the critical feedback of myself and other black female colleagues if it did not support her perspective or proposed course of action.

We began a heated disagreement in public, both of us speaking loudly, our voices hot with rage. One of the nasty sarcastic remarks I made declared: "Oh we are not doing sisterhood today: we are doing white supremacy." Leaving that encounter with my raging ego I felt confident I would never speak to her again. Thankfully, as time passed and the ego no longer controlled my emotions, I could recall the many occasions that we had stood in solidarity, the many moments we had shared the sweetness of life. In time we found our way both to forgiveness and reconciliation. For her it meant really learning more about how white supremacy can speak through us unconsciously. For her it meant really learning how to really trust the knowledge of black female colleagues. Throughout this conflict I was mindfully aware of the many moments when I had a choice either to be compassionate and hold onto our bond or to allow anger and blame to sever meaningful ties. We were both grateful that we lived the theory we teach and preach; we were both eager to celebrate anew that sisterhood is powerful.

Bringing the mindful awareness to bonding across differences keeps us ever cognizant of the reality that conflicts will happen, that even when we fear them we can and do learn to handle them. Most importantly, as in any relationship, we learn to grow and change. Conflicts in and of themselves do not make bonding better; it is how we work with the conflicts. Often white folks harbor tremendous fear that a person of color will label them racist. This fear seems even more magnified if the individual has been extremely attached to an image of themselves as anti-racist. If we drop for a time the focus on racism and acknowledge that we have all been raised to embrace the logic of white supremacy (this includes people of color), then we can accept this as a fundamental aspect of our psychic upbringing. We can accept that white supremacist thought and action, no matter how relative, was imprinted on all our consciousnesses early in life. Then we can share the common awareness that each of us has to critically examine the extent that early socialization continues to influence us and to identify the ways we have chosen to decolonize our minds. In *Parenting for Peace and Justice,* authors Kathleen and James McGinnis honestly name the need for critical self-examination as a necessary component of an anti-racist process: "We would suggest that the place to begin is with ourselves—our own attitudes, our behavior...Taking a look at our own attitudes about race can be frightening. There are times when we do not like what we see in ourselves, times when we have to admit we are not comfortable with our fear, questions, resentments, uneasiness....There is no magic formula for changing racial attitudes. Help comes in different forms, at different times, and from different sources." The willingness to self-evaluate is crucial to any process of unlearning racism and white supremacy.

Accepting that we have all been indoctrinated into white supremacist thinking allows us to let go of a shallow politics of blame. Instead we can focus on issues of responsibility and accountability. All the solidarity I have formed across difference is based on a foundation of accountability, a belief that no matter our socialization, ultimately we are responsible for the choices we make about what to believe and how to act. Again and again I learn in conversation with my white allies in struggle that many of them made the choice to be anti-racist in childhood. Respecting the reality that children can make such a serious ethical decision and commitment should remind us all that we have the power to transform our consciousness, our habits of being.

Everyone I encounter who is looking beyond race and racism, who remains committed to challenging and changing white supremacy, is guided by critical thinking. In our efforts to bond across differences, one lesson we learn early in the process is to not make assumptions about the nature of who people are, to not think we can know by looking at a surface reality. One of the most unique friendships of my life has happened between myself and a white "redneck" man, Eugene, who built the house I have in the Kentucky hills. When I asked the previous owners, who are white, if the builder would make changes, the man responded by stating that he was not sure that the builder would want to work for a black person. Reluctantly, he helped us connect. Apprehensive about going alone to the hills to meet Eugene, I asked an older white woman professor if she would join me.

When we met it was soon evident that this hardworking Kentucky hillbilly who lived in a hollow was deeply committed to living an open life where he felt free to bond across differences with people. By judging him on the basis of appearances and on class status, the white couple he first worked for never allowed themselves to know him beyond race and racism. They never had the opportunity to hear his story.

Certainly, active listening is essential to the process of learning and connecting across difference. When we stop making assumptions and allow folk the opportunity to share their backgrounds with us, to let us know how they see themselves, there is a much stronger will to connect. And that connection is central to the process of building community. Curiosity is a trait that strengthens all our efforts to meet across differences. In dominator culture most of us have been taught from childhood on that curiosity is dangerous. Even the common childhood expression "curiosity killed the cat" suggests to children that there is a problem with seeking knowledge beyond what is deemed acceptable. In my work I write about the place of "radical openness" as a useful standpoint to approach the world of difference and otherness.

Sharing humor is crucial to bonding across difference. Laughing together is always a way to intensify intimacy. When we can laugh at mistakes, laugh even in the midst of our tears, we affirm that what keeps us together is always more important than what can separate us. Laughter often serves as a powerful intervention when the issues we are confronting are hard and painful. It offers a way to change the channel, to let us "chill" for a moment and really cool down, returning to states of calmness that make communication possible. Shared laughter helps create the context for feelings of mutuality to emerge.

When the feminist movement was at its peak, there was so much talk about the need for equality. It was presented as a basis for sisterhood. Of course as women began to speak our differences we were exposed to all that made relationships between females unequal.

The theory had to change. Visionary feminists began to talk about the importance of mutuality, of a partnership. Using such a model as a basis for connection opened the possibility that there could be grave differences between people but that difference need not lead to domination. Knowing, for example, that a straight person has unearned heterosexual privilege can lead that person to mindful awareness about how to interact with gay folks in ways that affirm that all our identities are acceptable. Mutuality calls us to respect one another. Since the root meaning of the word *respect* is "to look at it," we can use our visions to learn one another, to see who we really are behind the mask of categories. We can move beyond difference.

My early childhood was spent in the hills of Kentucky. Mama's family were people from the backwoods. There was no welcoming of difference in our lives. We were taught to stay with the same and to fear the strange. Given that our world was one of racial apartheid, learning to fear white folks was crucial to survival. It compelled us to be ever vigilant. Even so, the hills were the only racially integrated places, poor whites living in isolated hollows where poor blacks also lived. It was there that I learned to be curious about folks not like myself, to move past fear. And in that movement I became someone my family saw as different. To them it was not "natural" to want to move beyond relations with family and kin and to connect with strangers.

Throughout my teen years I bonded with strangers who were, like me, deemed different because we shared a common outsider status. I learned that it was possible to make a soul connection with someone; to move past race and all the other estranging categories. Meeting across all that might divide us showed me that a life of diversity was a more meaningful life. Just recently, one of my white students shared that she felt fearful of her longing to move beyond race and bond with people of color. She fears that even that desire is a small manifestation of unearned white privilege. Not wanting her to be afraid of this longing, instead, I encouraged her to trust in her capacity to be critically vigilant. That means she has to trust her knowledge of dominator culture so that she can have faith in her own strategies of resistance.

We can all have confidence in our strategies of resistance when we see the positive ways our lives and our habits of being are changed. I trust the white folks with whom I am allied because of their commitment to peace and justice, to ending domination. It was this will to work for change that motivated their bonding across difference. And it is our shared longing to live in solidarity with one another that helps us forge sustained bonds of fellowship and camaraderie.

The practice of compassion is also central to peacemaking. It is our empathy with folks who are not like ourselves that breaks down barriers and allows bonds of connection to be formed. By always regarding each other with compassion we are able to accept not just that we all have our differences, but that we also all make mistakes. This is especially the case when bonding across race. No matter the depth of our commitment to change, there will still be moments of confusion. After years of working to challenge and change sexism, I now and then find myself thinking or behaving in a way that is not in tune with my beliefs. I find it difficult to see that within me there is still work to be done. However, as I show compassion toward my flawed and imperfect self, I am better able to accept the imperfections of others. Often we hurt each other even though there is no desire on our part to do harm.

Sadly, because so many individuals have been wounded by the practices of domination and have experienced severe trauma, we can trigger pain in others by making comments that we might think are funny or without serious intent. Recently, I was giving a lecture focused on Marable's biography of Malcolm X. I talked about the ways the biographer denigrated this leader for no apparent reasons. Speaking spontaneously I called attention to the book cover, stating that the image of Malcolm made him look "retarded." Afterward several colleagues, black and white, commented on the inappropriate nature of my description. Of course, like most folks who offend with casual spoken language, I insisted that I meant no harm, but when taking a moment to think about the issue I could see clearly how someone in the room with a disability who had been taunted and ridiculed with the tag "retarded" would be triggered by my off-hand comment. When I suggested to my colleagues that they should have critiqued me during the talk, they claimed to be too embarrassed on my behalf. To my way of thinking, it would have been a useful teaching moment. And even if there was no disabled person in the room it was still inappropriate language. The most appropriate response when we find we have inadvertently used the tools of domination to hurt is to hear the hurt and make amends.

In every relationship I have had with a white person who has unlearned white supremacy compassion has helped us be forgiving. We do not hold onto hurt or project past pain onto present encounters. Practicing forgiveness means there can always be reconciliation. When we build trust, we learn that we can take risks, make mistakes; and our bonds of intimacy and solidarity will stand firm. Even in the best of friendships where much is shared, there are times of conflict. Those are the times when our trust that the other person or person has our best interest at heart is affirmed.

Critical feedback is one of the ways we learn about how best to relate across boundaries. In the process of engaging one another critically we often find that the differences separating us are not as vital as the common experiences that connect us. If we are too focused on difference, we will neglect those shared realities. In the deepest bonds of my life that have moved beyond race what has connected us is something that mattered that we shared. With my friend Eugene we found common ground in our mutual obsession with houses and fast cars. Finding common ground does not erase conflicts that emerge from difference; it is just the strong foundation that lets us know again and again that we need not fear conflict, that we can constructively handle what comes our way.

Had I followed my family's insistence that I stay away from the "other," whomever that other might be, so much that is wonderful and marvelous would be absent from my life. Finding words to accurately share the comfort and solidarity that emerges when we work for change and bonding across our differences is no simple matter. Dominator culture wants us to lack a language to fully express the beauty and power of diversity. As we live our theory of beloved community we will become more and more able to find the words to express how peace and justice transforms, how love keeps us together.

13

Everyday Resistance: Saying No to White Supremacy

The bottom line of race and racism is white supremacy. One can be mindful of the impact of white supremacy while working consciously with mindful awareness to create a life where wholeness of self and identity stand as the powerful counter-hegemonic resistance to engulfment by racialized identity. Black folks, young and old, who are swept away by the idea of race and its concomitant anti-black racist agenda tend to end up seeing themselves as victims, living with depleting psychological states of fear and paranoia, states of mind that make coping in a predominately white world difficult, if not downright impossible.

Even though there is much awareness that daily white supremacist thinking and action are pervasive, there is little commentary about what folks can do to protect mind, body, and heart. To find any book that looks at the impact of television's biases in the direction of white supremacy on the minds of young black children would be a rare occurrence. And yet it is primarily television images which mirror white supremacist aesthetics that teach children about the relevance of skin color, that black skin is undesirable. Many single parents, female and male, allow excessive unscreened television watching as a means of caretaking when they want a break or are preoccupied with other household concerns. Even though I am a mindfully aware adult, one way that I shield myself from continuous white supremacist onslaught is by not watching television indiscriminately.

Black children cannot self-monitor what they watch. And no one is really checking to see the extent to which the images they see teach self-hate and diminish the possibility that they will create healthy self-esteem. Newton Minow and Craig LaMay in *Abandoned in the Wasteland: Children, Television, and the First Amendment* cautioned the American public about the psychological dangers of excessive indiscriminant television viewing and the need to provide a healthier television environment for children. While they did not write about the myriad ways television teaches the values of white supremacy or the ways non-white folks are depicted, they did call attention to the reality that black children spent more hours watching television than any other group of children. Given the struggle to end racism, it would seem essential and necessary for there to be an abundance of literature critically examining the impact of television on the development of racial identity and racial consciousness, especially self-help psychological works aimed at a mass audience. Yet no such abundance exists. And even when a liberal president like Clinton can call for a national discussion of race, such discussions, when they take place, rarely focus on the impact of white supremacist culture on children, especially black children. All children need to be shielded from the harmful constructions of race and racism normalized in our society. All children need to be given guidance when watching television.

No doubt there are few parents in our society today who outspokenly teach their children white supremacist thinking and practice. Those white folks who want their children to engage with white supremacy as well as those who do not can rest assured that the pedagogy of white supremacy will be learned by watching television. And what is learned there will be mirrored in the larger culture. In their insightful book *Parenting for Peace and Justice,* Kathleen and James McGinnis contend: "White children constantly receive messages from the culture that say to be white is to be somehow superior to people of color.... White children come naturally to accept white as a norm or standard and to see other skin colors as deviations from the norm, and therefore deviations from real people.... This situation gives white children a false sense of self and hampers them in functioning harmoniously with people of different races." Learning critical thinking at an early age can help young children resist the messages.

When Jerry Mander's book *Four Arguments for the Elimination of Television* was first published in the late 1970s, it included a chapter titled "The Colonization of Experience." In this chapter, he warns viewers that "television encourages separation," explaining that even though television offers an experience that can be had by everyone at the same time, it must reduce the diversity of experience so as to control everyone's awareness. I grew up at a time in our nation's history when it was rare to see images of black folks on television. Just turning on one's television set created awareness of the omnipresence of racial apartheid, of white supremacy. The fictive world of television was a white world designed to meet the needs of white viewers. In those days when black folks watched television, we rarely thought we were seeing any representation that had meaning for our lives or that mirrored our values; how could it when our ways of responding to white supremacy were counter-hegemonic. Just as the real racist white folks were out to get us, to colonize our minds and imaginations, so were the real white screen images. Even black girls in rural southern settings knew that television then was not our friend and today is clearly a serious enemy.

Ironically, during the sixties, civil rights anti-racist protest brought televised black images into every home as riots were documented, and yet these images no way challenged racist stereotypes. Indeed, mass audience fascination with these images highlighted the reality that black images could be represented on television, attracting viewers of all races without in any way being anti-racist. Even though more and more black folks were shown on television, the roles they played and play continue to be defined by racist biases, by negative stereotypes. What is most amazing is the reality that despite the shift in our intellectual and academic understanding of white supremacy, race, and racism, representations of blackness on the television screen and in movies are as negatively stereotyped as they were during periods of racial apartheid.

Even moderately positive interventions like *The Cosby Show* have morphed into shows that have more in common with nineteenth-century minstrelsy. It's ironic that there appears to be progress because more black folks are image-makers and black actors have more jobs than ever before, but their roles in no way challenge racist perceptions. The recent phenomenal success of *The Help* (both movie and book), which purports to give us a fictive account of race relations between white female employers and black domestics in the segregated world of Mississippi in the 1960s, epitomizes a disturbing trend. On the surface it appears that the topic of the film is daring, that it will examine deep historical conflicts between women as created by social constructions of race and racism; yet, in reality, this history of suffering and trauma is brought to us as slapstick tragicomedy and farce and the same old racist understanding prevails. It offers no hope of an anti-racist world where white and black females can hope to construct better relationships with one another, relationships that will not be based on culturally accepted paradigms of domination rather than a partnership model.

Ultimately, the book and film suggest that folks are happier when they bond with folks just like themselves. The underlying message is integrate to segregate; for when the story ends, the races are all neatly in their place. White children receive affirming care from adult black females, and black children are taught by these same females to cope with lives where they will receive little or no care, where they can only hope to be "the help." There has been no contemporary film that has angered and disturbed black females as deeply as *The Help*. For many grown black females, especially those of us who were raised in a racially segregated world where our mothers worked as domestics in white homes, the historical inaccuracy of the film, as well as the profoundly dehumanizing depictions of black womanhood, of black families, triggered psychological distress. Folks who were traumatically victimized by this exploitation and oppressive system of racial apartheid, either directly as victims or indirectly as witnesses, found the images triggered post-traumatic stress.

Clearly, reading the book was quite a different experience than watching the movie. Reading the book, one could easily distance oneself via disassociation. Since the book was poorly written, often with seemingly poor paraphrases of already published works by black and white females, it could easily be dismissed, unlike the film. Visual images impact the psyche in far more visceral ways than the written word. Triggering memories of trauma, of the disrespect and contempt white females have shown black females in the past and present, it is no wonder that some black women hurt watching this film; it felt to them as though they were being violated yet again. Still other black females fearful of being hurt refused to see the film, confident in their assumption that they did not want the negative images represented to be imprinted on their minds, consciously or unconsciously. Although I freely chose to read the book, I would not have chosen to watch the movie. Like *Precious,* I knew there would be images and words I would not want in my head. As Jerry Mander declared years ago: "It is possible to speak through media directly into people's heads and…leave images inside that can cause people to do what they might otherwise never have thought to do." Not wanting to "hear" or "see" cinematic messages of *The Help* I resisted seeing the film until placed on several conference panels where it was a topic of discussion.

Critical thinking helped me to approach both film and movie with the appropriate psychological detachment. While I did not feel "hurt" by the negative images, given the choice I would not have consumed these commodities.

White supremacist thinking is seeping into the heads of children who cannot protect their minds from the ideas entering their consciousness through mass media, especially television. Of course, magazines are as much a culprit as television (fortunately children, especially those who cannot read, are not as exposed to print media). A critical examination of any magazine in our nation will show that the aesthetics of white supremacy prevail. This is equally true of magazines marketed specifically to black people/people of color. Determining value by focusing on skin color is as much a part of black life today as it was in the nineteenth century. Fair skin and long hair are still viewed as the most desirable characteristics. While all females in our culture are indoctrinated with white supremacist aesthetics (witness the proliferation of hair salons that do nothing but color hair blonde), black females are especially obsessed with undergoing whatever assault on the body is needed to produce lighter skin, long straight hair.

Although most black folks acknowledge the extent to which white supremacy shapes collective thinking about self-valuation, very few folk act as though anything can be done to change white supremacist thought and action. Chris Rock's documentary film *Good Hair* is a perfect example of how the taboo subject of hair and race can be addressed with no critical commentary. Even though the film shows the pain young black children endure when their hair is straightened, the film never suggests these practices should be viewed as assaultive or abusive and thus stopped. At the end of the film when Chris Rock is asked whether not he will support his daughters if they want to straighten their hair, he responds that it is a matter of their personal choice. Yet the film has already shown that personal choice cannot be separated from white supremacist thinking, from imperialist exploitation (the film documents the way women in India are tricked to cut their hair so it may be sold for extensions and weaves).

Assimilating into the dominator culture is perceived by most black people/people of color to be the path to success. As long as white supremacist thinking and practice covertly and/or unconsciously teach folk that they must support and perpetuate this system if they are to make it into the mainstream, race and racism will not end. We begin the process of challenging and changing white supremacy by becoming more aware, by refusing to remain silent victims. Kathleen and James McGinnis suggest that to create an environment which teaches respect for everyone we must "encourage and actively promote a deep respect for racial and cultural differences and a capacity for rejoicing in and learning from, rather than merely tolerating those differences." When we call attention to the conditions needed for the growth of healthy self-esteem, work that must begin with childhood, we help create an environment where white supremacy can be challenged in all its many manifestations. Turning our collective gaze away from old assumptions about race and racism, refusing to see the problem as solely about direct discrimination or overt harmful acts, opens the space where white supremacy as it is expressed in everyday racism can be called out, critically examined, and eliminated.

14

Against Mediocrity

My love affair with books began with reading, not with writing. Long before I ever began to write, books were changing my view of the world, giving me information, and painting pictures of places and ways of being that were way different from the narrow confines of the life I lived within—transforming me. I am where I am today not because I am a writer, but first and foremost because I am a reader. In the biblical Book of Revelations there is a passage which declares "blessed is one that reads." In the fifties, when I was beginning my life as a reader, it was a struggle to find works by black writers, and so when I found them I read whatever they wrote. Devouring these writers, feeding my soul hunger (the heartbeat of love is recognition), it did not matter how many awesome and wonderful non-black writers were out there. The knowledge that there were black writers out there did not help me to become a writer, but rather to be comfortable with myself as a writer.

This foundation of self-love and self-esteem emerging from pro-found respect for the historical legacy of black writers in no way kept me from continuing to love and respect all great and meaningful literature, nor did it stop my reading of and learning from the work of many writers who were at their core white supremacist in thought and vision. One of the first books by a black writer I read came from my father's bookshelf (a consistent reader, a critically thinking working man). It was James Baldwin's *The Fire Next Time*. I could not have asked for a better literary mentor than Baldwin—witty, radical, transgressive, a sexual renegade, he embodied it all. And there he was writing to his nephew telling him that the "heart of the matter is here." He writes, "You were born where you were born and faced the future that you faced because you were black and for no other reason. The limits of your ambition were, thus, expected to be set forever. You were born into a society which spelled out with brutal clarity, and in as many ways as possible, that you were a worthless human being. You were not expected to aspire to excellence: you were expected to make peace with mediocrity." This letter to his nephew was offered as warning, as caution.

How many of you have read Baldwin, not just one paragraph or one essay, but really read and studied James Baldwin? How many of you have heeded his reminder that our striving for excellence in the world of words as readers and writers is itself an act of political resistance? At work I remind readers again and again that our right to read and write as black folks is a legacy of liberation struggle. People died for this.

In a world where we understand the power of words to set us free or to bind us forever to the mediocre, the substandard, the junk food trashy stuff that will never nourish our souls, we must as black readers and writers be ever vigilant. We must demand a diversity of work, work that is serious and playful, work that is trashy, cheap, vulgar. I like that pulp fiction has its place. I want to see more black mystery writers, more tacky romances. However, we do not want to allow unenlightened market forces (the mindset of imperialist white supremacist capitalist patriarchy) to determine the nature of what we read and write. In a world where white writers often gain great status and are taken seriously when they write about race, black writers are still worried that if they talk about stuff having to do with race they will be seen as not good enough, not serious, too emotional.

Even liberal white writers cannot resist imposing on black writers this weight. Receiving the Jerusalem Prize at the International Book Fair on 9 May 2001, Susan Sontag (a writer I have read, studied, admired) endeavored in her talk to speak to the necessity of writers not getting bogged down in propagandistic political polemic, urging them to maintain the integrity of vision and craft. She declared, "It's one thing to volunteer, stirred by the imperatives of conscious or of interest, to engage in public debate and public action. It's another to produce opinions—moralistic sound-bites on demand." But she said: "the writer ought not to be an opinion machine." The example she then offers of the denigration of writerly craft evokes the issue of race.

She stated: "As a black poet in my country put it, when reproached by some fellow African-Americans for not writing poems about the indignities of racism: 'A writer is not a jukebox.'" While her point that writers should never write on demand, playing the tune anyone wants to hear, might be true, it's troubling that this writer who in the vast majority of her work never mentions any black writers (notice the black poet she refers to has no name) manages to use an analogy that implies black writers who write about racism are not "real" writers, and racism is maybe not a real issue, a serious issue. Of course, it's ironic that Sontag is giving her talk in Jerusalem, a place where the politics of white supremacy, imperialism, and colonialism continue to rule the day. Reading her words in this new millennium I am struck by the use that she makes of this anonymous black poet, who has no gender, no name—only a racialized identification. Only a few paragraphs later when she quotes Roland Barthes, he is not a white European man, he is a writer with a name, and yet the comments she quotes are no more substantial than the words of the anonymous black writer.

My people, my people: here we are in the new millennium and we must fight for our right to become and to be seen as serious writers and thinkers. We are still fighting to have our words taken seriously no matter our subject matter, and yet we are still fighting not to be denigrated, not to be seen as mediocre when we write about race and racism. When I read Sontag's words I wonder who the black writers are that she reads and takes seriously, especially the writers of non-fiction. Many of the white readers I know read no black writers, or when they do read, they read novels. We are still living in a world that does not take the work of black writers seriously enough, or that can take our words seriously only if we strip ourselves of any racial awareness, if we write from the perspective deemed universal.

Many black readers and other non-black readers do not choose to seek out the work of black writers. Note how many times you read a white writer, female or male, talking about which writer's work has meant a lot to them and they will mention almost no black writers. There is still so much we need to read about blackness. There is so much that we need to hear from black folks about every subject imaginable. Everything that we need to read and write about is not necessarily going to fill a book that will bring in vast sums of money in sales. We need to be mindful of all the work that is not yet available to us—books for teens, more memoirs that tell the truth, biographies of writers and other folks that are slow to come to the public's attention, of Audre Lorde, of Pat Parker, of Essex Hemphill, of Marlon Riggs.

In our reading and our writing we must refuse to make peace with mediocrity. We must demand excellence. Prophetically, Baldwin tells us: "We should certainly know by now that it is one thing to overthrow a dictator or repel an invader and quite another thing really to achieve a revolution. Time and time and time again, the people discover that they have merely betrayed themselves into the hands of yet another Pharaoh, who...will not let them go." Let us be ever vigilant as readers and as writers. Let us recognize, as Baldwin did, that we are living "in an age of revolution." Think of all the books on all subjects having to do with black experience that you want and need to read. Think about what it means for us not to have just one book on a subject of relevance to our lives written by one black writer but to have many books with diverse perspectives on the same subject. If we want to be part of a revolution, if we want to resist the tyranny of mediocrity then we must see excellence—the striving for excellence in our reading and writing—as essential political resistance.

15

Black
Self-Determination

Current focus on black thinkers and public intellectuals has led many folks to speculate whether we are seeing a resurgence of W.E.B. DuBois's vision of a talented tenth, which he initially defined as "leadership of the Negro race in America by a trained few." However, contemporary thinkers do not call attention to the memorial address (Boulé Journal, 15 October 1948) wherein DuBois critiqued his earlier vision of a talented tenth. In this address he acknowledges that when he suggested the need for a talented group that would spearhead racial uplift, he simply assumed that these individuals would be committed to the collective well-being of black people—that would want to use their talents to benefit everywhere. He contends:

> I assumed that with knowledge, sacrifice would automatically follow. In my youth and idealism, I did not realize that self-ishness is more natural than sacrifice....When I came out of college into the world of work, I realized that it was quite possible that my plan of training a talented tenth might put in

control and power, a group of selfish, self-indulgent, well-to-do men, whose basic interest in solving the Negro problem was personal; personal freedom and unhampered enjoyment and use of the world, without any real care, or certainly no arousing care, as to what became of the mass of American Negroes, or the mass of any people.

This powerful declaration made in 1948 awesomely and prophetically describes the current relationship of today's black "talented tenth" to the masses of black people. Indeed one cannot simply evoke the term *black genius* and assume that there is any direct correlation between black people in the diaspora who possess exceptional intellectual ability and liberatory efforts to create a local or global cultural context that affirms and sustains collective black self-determination. Significantly, the word *genius* also means "a person who strongly influences for good or ill the character, conduct, or destiny of a person, place, or thing." More often than not the black genius in the United States has little or no contact with masses of black people. This is especially true if that genius has been nurtured in predominantly white educational institutions. Even though individuals whose talents have been nurtured in these environments can actively choose as an insurgent act of resistance to direct their work toward masses of black people, this is rarely the case, largely because the mechanisms of reward, whether via accruing recognition, status, or monetary gain, remain highest for those who turn their backs on the masses. By this statement I do not mean to imply that black people trained at black institutions are inherently more inclined to direct their work toward black self-determination.

Irrespective of whether they are predominantly white or black, academic institutions are by nature and direction structurally conservative. Their primary function is to produce a professional managerial class that will serve the interests of the existing social and political status quo. Given that the ideologies of imperialist white supremacist capitalist patriarchy form the founding principles of culture in the United States, ways of thinking and being that are taught via mass socialization in educational institutions, it should be evident that the fundamental concerns of the academy in general are at odds with any efforts to affirm black self-determination.

Currently the vast majority of black academics, writers, and/or critical thinkers, whether they pitch their work to a predominantly white or black audience (or some combination of race), do not choose to be dissident voices challenging imperialist white supremacist capitalist patriarchy. In those cases where an individual begins writing with the hope that work they contribute will make them famous and/ or produce huge monetary profit, from the onset this self-interested foundation will preclude identification with a concern for black self-determination or the well-being of masses of black people. It is more likely that their identification with blackness will be toward solidarity with black folks who share their upwardly mobile class aspirations. Indeed, if we return to DuBois's critique of the vision of a black talented tenth, the solidarity of black genius, it is evident that he began to see that desires for individual upward mobility within the existing class structure of this society, especially as it pertained to profit-making and status, would ultimately mean that the class aspirations of this professional managerial group would lead them to betray the interests of the black masses.

More than ever before in our political history black people in the United States confuse reformist efforts for civil rights and equity with agendas for decolonization and liberation. While reforms are important, they do not constitute radical interventions aimed at transforming society in ways that ensure the collective well-being of masses of black people. Let's be clear: black capitalism is not black self-determination. In the last ten years we have witnessed an unprecedented commodification of "blackness" in relationship to academic and/or popular discourses about race and culture. On the academic front, where the interest of market forces converges with bourgeoning mainstream cultural interests in reading about blackness, there is an ongoing infusion of works by and about black writers that is almost entirely divorced from any collective efforts to galvanize masses of black people.

Those individual black people who have come to power either in the academy or outside of it as cultural brokers of "blackness" and who have not linked their work to any efforts to enhance the well-being of masses of black people can do so precisely because there is no network of accountability that critically examines the impact of this work. Often these individuals police and actively seek to delegitimize and silence the voices of dissident black genius, which both affirms black self-determination and consistently opposes imperialist white supremacist capitalist patriarchy. In my own experience using mainstream media, black individuals of talent and genius have been more outspoken than any other group in devaluing my work. (For example, Stanley Crouch referred to me as a "terrier with attitude"; Adolph Reed described me in *The Village Voice* as "little more than [a] hustler"; and the most vicious trashing came from my colleague Michele Wallace—none of these individuals referred to the content of my books.) There can be no meaningful discussion of black genius in relation to black self-determination without the recognition of political and social differences that place us at odds with one another and/or the way in which an ethics of competition may lead us to devalue one another's work even if we do not differ politically.

Concurrently, the patriarchal mindset of the culture as a whole colludes with the intentionality of individual patriarchal men who seek to maintain a lineage of intellectual genius that always makes it seem that men have been the most significant political visionaries. Again, an example: the written text for a PBS series on black genius evokes a continuum of black genius that is exclusively male, declaring "DuBois shall meet Garvey here" or that black genius is present "in the mother-child, and it is in Mandela." While the historical lineage of visible black genius in relation to radical discourses of colonialism and white supremacy was primarily, if not exclusively, male, this is no longer the case. In our times, some of the most radical critiques of imperialist white supremacist capitalist patriarchy are emerging from black women thinkers whose work is consistently devalued and/or rendered less visible.(e.g., Lorraine Hansberry, Audre Lorde, Toni Cade Bambara). Usually the work of visionary contemporary black women thinkers has a more radical edge precisely because it includes a critique of patriarchy while simultaneously insisting on a union between theory and practice which privileges the experiential as the site where change and transformation is registered.

I want to conclude these comments by giving an example of work I have completed which was directed toward the enhancement of the collective well-being of black people and the positing of another alternative strategy for healing the pain in our everyday lives. First I would like to talk about the process by which I chose to write and publish the book *Sisters of the Yam: Black Women and Self-Recovery*. It became increasingly clear to me that much of the feminist theory I was writing from, a perspective that included race, sex, and class. was not being read by enough non-academic readers, and especially black readers. When I looked at the types of books that had broader appeal, it was soon evident that self-help books, even those written with primarily a white audience in mind, attracted numerous black women readers. Since I was serious about wanting to share with a broad audience of black females the knowledge that I felt I had discovered and which had assisted me in my process of decolonization and self-actualization, I chose to incorporate this thinking in a self-help book.

In keeping with earlier comments, let me state that academic colleagues of all races advised me against writing such a book, suggesting that it would further de-legitimize me as an academic/intellectual. This is why I stress that we must choose whether to direct our work toward the empowerment of masses of black people all the while recognizing that what we choose is political and will have consequences. Indeed, I would suggest that black thinkers who try to speak to masses of people, especially to promote black self-determination, will definitely risk ridicule and de-legitimatization. When I first sought a publisher for this book, I was told that it was not clear who the audience would be, that black women do not buy this type of book. (Even though no one could give a concrete example of a book like this that had failed to succeed). They could not because self-help books in general do not call attention to politics and certainly not to the way in which systems of domination (e.g., white supremacist capitalist patriarchy) create the context for mental illness. Since no one in the publishing process (except me) felt confident that there was an audience for this book, I received a relatively small advance to write it. Despite few reviews and little attention given it in the mainstream press, it was a success. It succeeded because it offered strategies for healing that could be applied to everyday life.

Currently, I am writing about the extent to which hedonistic materialism creates tremendous pain in the daily lives of African Americans across class. Much stress in daily life is caused by constant feelings of lack created by the absence of material plenty and unrequited yearnings stimulated by fantasies of wealth and privilege. To this end when black people across class commit ourselves to living simply as a way of breaking the stress caused by unrelenting hedonistic desire for material objects (that is to say, objects that are not needed for survival and essential well-being), we can find a sense of peace and well-being. For those of us who are materially privileged but spend our lives in discontentment because we are perpetually consuming and hoarding, often spreading the message to less privileged black people that their lives have no meaning if they do not have the freedom to fulfill hedonistic desires for material goods, then it is equally meaningful to practice living simply, to redistribute our resources, to engage philanthropy that enhances the collective well-being of black people.

Many black people live simply because they have no access to material plenty. Rather than seeing the experience of living simply as a gesture of inter-being which enables them to live in greater harmony with masses of people on the planet, they spend their days in mental anguish because of their inability to fulfill hedonistic material longings. If we study the lives of southern black people who lived well during periods of depression, we see that they had lives of sustained well-being because they were committed to living simply (for instance, eating healthy food they grew themselves) and clinging to spiritual traditions which emphasized substantive values (integrity of one's word, right action and livelihood) over fantasies of hedonistic materialism.

The embrace of a strategy for living simply in everyday life, irrespective of one's level of material privilege, would enable masses of black people to eliminate unnecessary suffering caused by the unrelenting desire for material excess. If masses of black people embraced the philosophy of living simply as a way to counter some of the genocidal abuse in our lives fostered by imperialist white supremacist capitalist patriarchy, we would also be uniting our struggle with that of most people on the planet who are daily grievously victimized by the material excesses of society. There is a bumper sticker which reads "live simply so that others may simply live." When made as a political decision, the choice to embrace living simply can liberate and enhance our collective well-being, healing and soothing some of the pain in everyday life.

16

Ending Racism: Working for Change

I am especially lucky to have been born in the early part of the 1950s, for I was able to witness firsthand during my girlhood racial apartheid and that period in our nation's history where sexist gender roles were reinscribed, as well as the marvelous cultural revolution in our society that was created by the civil rights and feminist movements. Making the transition from girlhood into young womanhood at a time when our nation was in transition—breaking with patterns of domination and the racialized colonialism that had characterized the conquest and terrorization of Native American Indians and then later their African counterparts. Rebellion and revolution, the will to transform myself and demand transformation within the country and culture where I am most at home is my birthright, the legacy of the times in which I was born and grew into mature womanhood. While there are many ways we learn, many epistemologies (ways of knowing), we all know that experience coupled with awareness and critical reflections about what is happening around us and why it is happening is one of life's great teachers. To have been raised during our nation's period of legally sanctioned apartheid, when so many rights were denied us based on the color of our skin, to stand before stores that would not allow us to enter, to see the closing of our beloved black schools, and to board in the wee hours of the morning the buses that took us away from the world that was most familiar to us and into a strange, horribly racist world where we would always be treated as second-class citizens, never the equals of the white children who were our peers and only sometimes, on rare occasions, our allies and our friends, was to know firsthand the anguish and the pain, the fear and the subordination. But it was also to know firsthand the sweetness of solidarity, of struggle, of standing in resistance. To have lived in the fifties when the violence against women and children that I saw in our communities went unnoticed and uncared about, to know that women stayed with men because they could not get jobs, not have bank accounts, and credit cards, all these were the ways I learned about sexism and patriarchy. Living to see serious change, being a part of both the struggle for racial and gender justice, and seeing profound changes occur have given me a foundation of hope that sustains and strengthens my activism.

Sadly, before the onset of the civil rights and contemporary feminist movements, war, more than any other cultural force, rendered more complex social constructions of female roles and identity in relation to work and sexuality. Black soldiers moving away from the narrow identities and borders that contained them in the United States brought back from their journeys a new sense of themselves and their rights. They came home believing if they could fight and die for human rights and freedom in foreign lands then they deserved those rights here at home, too; they deserved to be free.

My father fought in an all-black infantry in World War II. On the wall in our home was the picture of him and his troop with one white face, that of the man in charge, the man in high rank; black men could fight for their country but they could not lead other men in war. Just as my father had been told that black males did not have the brains and skills to be quarterbacks, he had been told they did not have the brains and skills to lead other men in war, to map strategy and direct moves. My father, like many other black men, returned home from the war silent and bitter, believing it was better not to speak about racial segregation and the atrocious treatment of black soldiers by their white counterparts. He came home bitter about the conditions of life here in this country. He came home thinking of soldiers as dehumanized beings capable of all manner of evil. He did not want to speak about his time away. He did not want to show his passport or tell stories about the foreign lands he had visited. He did not want to remember. His one tribute to that time of his life was the hanging of a photo—him and his infantry—an array of young black male faces.

To have witnessed the profound cultural revolution in our nation as changes happened that make racial and gender justice more common, more a reality and not simply a dream, I cannot give up hope, even though it is clear that we are a nation that is daily reneging on its promise to end racism and white supremacy, that is daily stripping women of hard-earned equal rights. As much as we are theoretically a nation that speaks about democracy with pride, a nation wherein many citizens like to feel there is freedom and justice for all, we are more essentially a nation that has enshrined patterns of unjust, corrupt inequality that are longstanding. The very same greed for material advancement which characterized Columbus's journey to the so-called new world, the slaughter and colonization of many indigenous people so that Europe could expand its power, threatens to take the lives of people of color in our nation, and black people in particular. Enlightened people of color/black people now know far more than our ancestors ever did about the extent to which greed and the desire of the few to put in place and maintain an unjust and inequitable economic system was at the heart of the conquest of native people, the enslavement of Africans, and the indentured servitude of poor whites; the culture of domination in the United States has never been simply about xenophobia or white supremacy.

For a time in our nation's history, greed co-existed with visions of justice and freedom for all. These progressive visions, which were and are the heartbeat of democracy, provided a system of beliefs, morals, and values that were the foundation of critical interventions which led to the formation of a culture of resistance where domination, exploitation, and oppression were challenged and opposed. This spirit of resistance has been the foundation of all movements for social justice in our society. It has been the bedrock of our hope in the midst of suffering. Despite the legacy of struggle, of commitment to freedom and justice, we are witnessing at this time a consolidated attempt on the part of combined forces of domination—what many of us consistently and courageously call imperialist white supremacist capitalist patriarchy—to kill this spirit of resistance, and in the process create a culture without hope, a culture wherein the belief that materialism is all that matters and the belief that the politics of greed is the only real foundation needed to give life meaning will reign supreme. This culture is a breeding ground for fascism. Right now we are witnessing a resurgence of white supremacy, of Nazism, of all manner of holocaust enacted in the name of racial and ethnic purity globally.

In the past, among citizens of the United States, the will to resist injustice emerged most often among those individuals whose religious beliefs were the foundation of their activism, enabling them to courageously stand and challenge racism, materialism, sexism, and homophobia. When we look at the history of civil rights and the black liberation struggle, it is evident that the vast majority of our visionary leaders and activists, whether famous or unknown, found their strength to struggle within the context of efforts to embody in theory and practice the tenets of spiritual faith rooted in love and a will to end domination (for Martin Luther King and Septima Clark, this faith was Christianity; for Malcolm X, it was Islam; and among our white allies in struggle, Christian and Judaic faiths have enhanced political concerns with justice). This is rarely the case today. Indeed the more progressive an individual's political view of our society the more likely s/he is to be agnostic or atheist. A vast majority of progressive folks who believe in god and/or a higher power in no way link their beliefs to organized religious tradition and ritual.

Religion, and in particular fundamentalism, is one of the primary tools used by conservative individuals who wish to perpetuate and sustain white supremacist capitalist patriarchy. Radical progressive religious voices are not as unified as the religious right. The right has garnered the services of mass media to send its message globally. Irrespective of their color, television evangelists share conservative perspectives. Ironically, while new age spirituality, complete with politically informed revisioning of gender, is on the rise, popular gurus say little or nothing about ending racism and sexism. And much of the writing valorizes prosperity in such a way as to make wealth and well-being synonymous. Among young people across the nation, fundamentalist religious thinking—whether coming from Christianity, Islam, Buddhism, and so forth—appeals because it offers absolute guidelines that promise stability in a world where everything is constantly shifting. At a small liberal arts college with a Christian religious affiliation, young white students stand to tell me "that if we would just accept that we are all one in Christ" racism would not exist. At a hip-hop panel with famous young black entertainers, an old testament patriarchal god of discipline and punishment is evoked as the ultimate judge and arbiter of human behavior—and little attention is given to individual responsibility for moral and ethical choices. Both groups are fiercely homophobic and use Christianity to justify their anti-gay sentiments. Fundamentalist religious thinking has undergirded practically every major act of racial terrorism we have witnessed in the last few years in this society and much of the racial terrorism which precedes it. Progressive religious beliefs which extol the virtues of compassion, a love ethic, and sharing of resources are needed if we are to rekindle a spirit of resistance where domination is always challenged and opposed. The radical religious left needs to come together and create a public voice for itself.

Religion is important because it is there that many folks learn the western metaphysical dualism—the notion of world divided between the good and the bad, the chosen and the unchosen, the worthy and the unworthy, the blacks and the whites—that is the philosophical foundation for white supremacy and other forms of domination. As long as this thinking serves as the foundation for how most people think about life (in neat binaries) then it will be impossible to eradicate racism. White supremacist capitalist patriarchy thrives on the core dualistic thinking that is the foundation of all systems of domination.

Throughout my work I emphasize that it is more useful for everyone (especially black people/people of color) to think in terms of white supremacy rather than racism, because we usually associate racism with overt discriminatory acts of aggression by whites against blacks, whereas white supremacy addresses the ideological and philosophical foundations of racism. As a term it encompasses the anti-black sentiments many blacks have, the internalized racism. For example: a black mother who teaches her children that they are beautiful only if they are fair skinned and have straight hair is not engaged in an overt discriminatory act, but she is perpetuating white supremacy. She is attacking the self-esteem of her children and thus preparing them for victimization. Let me emphasize that this same mother might be utterly outraged if whites attempted to discriminate against her child on the basis of color.

Nothing has undermined the power of black people to be self-determining more than negative self-esteem. Many black folks raised in the apartheid south under materially lacking conditions (including profound poverty) learned healthy esteem and were able to change their lot in life both mental health wise and materially because of a sound foundation of "loving blackness." The absence of black images from white supremacist capitalist patriarchal mass media pre-1960 was on one hand a sign of the persistence of racial discrimination and apartheid but on the other hand it meant that black people were not daily bombarded with negative racist representations. Structural racial integration with no fundamental change in white supremacist thinking and values has simply meant that black people, though "integrated" into various arenas of mainstream life over time, were and still are seen as inferior. Most white Americans do not live in neighborhoods with black folks, work with any large number of us, attend predominately black churches, schools, and so forth. Real estate continues to be a business so informed by the politics of white supremacy as to ensure the continuation of an ipso facto racial apartheid. To this day our legal system makes it so difficult to prove that racial discrimination in housing takes place that hardly anyone bothers to contest the many instances where it occurs. Not to mention that part of why this contestation does not occur is due to black folks' deep fear of white racial terrorism and violence. After all, we know no incidence where black folks have bombed buildings to murder innocent white children or anybody else. Now, the stereotypes that undergird these beliefs do not correspond to the actual lives and thoughts of black people, but there is a total correspondence between what they convey and the common images of black people in mass media.

Elsewhere I have written extensively about the extent to which legalized racial apartheid created a cultural context wherein black folks were conditioned by circumstances of exploitation and oppression to question media images. That sharp critical interrogation began to cease when mainstream media became more racially integrated, despite the fact that many of the images portrayed were more profoundly racist and stereotypical than those in the early white supremacist propaganda film *Birth of a Nation*. The failure of black folks to remain collectively vigilant about the way we are represented in mass media has resulted in collusion with white supremacy. The vast majority of images reinforce either conventional stereotypes or the notion that black people are only good when they are serving the interests of white folks—whether as mammy, maid, prostitute, or good sidekick. When there are radically new images that challenge conventional stereotypes, they tend to be so few and far between they do not successfully intervene on the racist status quo.

Now, clearly white racism cannot be seen as the only factor in the production of images of blacks in mass media which reinforce white supremacy, for these images could not exist without the collusion of black folks who play the roles. To understand black complicity we need to highlight the link between white supremacy capitalism and the politics of greed. I have written elsewhere about the enormous grief and despair felt by black people when major leaders for civil rights were assassinated. The psychological despair that racism would never end, that justice could not prevail, that white people would not divest of white supremacy and racism was a perfect breeding ground for nihilism. Clearly we must reject any analysis of black life in America that would have us believe that nihilistic thinking is solely the outcome of poverty. During the poorest years of economic depression in this nation, black folks were not nihilistic. Poverty in and of itself, no matter how extreme, does not lead to nihilism. In many of the poorest countries in the world children have better self-esteem than children in more affluent societies.

Psychological depression is one consequence of traumatic racist assault coupled with despair about whether racism can be challenged and changed, which has troubled the collective psyche of black Americans. Where once our spirit of resistance had been fueled by hope, a love ethic rooted in compassion and forgiveness, the energy of the late sixties shaped by militaristic patriarchal black males, many of whom had pathologically low self-esteem which proclaimed violence and coercion as the best means of change, led to the decline of a humanitarian value-based civil rights struggle for justice, which ultimately lowered morale. When assertions of force were met with even more force (the assassination of King, Malcolm X, the destruction of the Black Panther Party), the message black folks received was that justice would never be a reality.

These events left masses of black folks with two choices: despair or collusion with the existing social structure. Depression and despair made the setting ripe for widespread addiction. Addiction brought to black communities a greed-based drug economy sanctioning dehumanization and violence. It created the context for black flight on the part of the materially privileged. Most predominately black communities in the United States were made up of diverse classes, and prior to recent racial integration in real estate markets, more wealthy black folks lived in black communities. Bourgeois lifestyles and habits of being set the standards. Education was valued as the primary vehicle of racial uplift. Once the drug economy and lack of employment opportunities (unemployed folks are more prone to depression—have more time on their hands, etc.) created war zone type–communities, only the underclass and the low-income working-class people remained. Black communities which had previously been safe neighborhoods were rendered unsafe. As a nation, as black thinkers, we have yet to produce a large body of work that examines and challenges the impact of widespread addiction on the disintegration of black communities spiritually, physically, and materially. This is holocaust, protracted, slow, invisible. And it is not caused by economics, by poverty.

The politics of greed informs masses of poor and working-class black folks' passive acceptance of life-threatening drug economies into diverse black communities. Throughout this nation, despair about the possibility that the world could change, that people could live in peace and harmony, that there could be justice and freedom for all led many people to embrace the consumer capitalist message that you are what you can buy—and that all pain can be escaped with the proper drug, whether it be alcohol, heroin, crack, or shopping. By the early eighties, masses of Americans were turning their back on the American dream of democracy and justice and turning toward a view of life where money is god, and consumption, paradise.

Many black leaders continue to act as though the collective crisis of black America can be solved by money. In an article in *Emerge* magazine focusing on black academics at Harvard, Henry Louis Gates spoke of his desire to see more black folks enter the middle class. Implicit in this assertion is the notion that acquiring more money improves life. Yet the black bourgeois and members of the ruling class wealthy in this society who are black have been among that group most invested in destructive color caste, looking down upon and showing contempt for the poor, pushing the notion that you are what you buy (and that's all that matters). More and more, mainstream society, particularly white Americans, are giving testimony that material affluence alone does not give life meaning. In our society, life-threatening addictions are as widespread among those groups with economic privilege as among the poor, and so is domestic violence (incest, rape, etc.). The difference is these groups have available resources—therapists, mental health care facilities, excellent medical care to confront their dilemmas and to find the place of healing if they so desire. I think it is important to refuse to resist both patriarchal and capitalist thinking that insists the acquisition of greater sums of money is the only way to improve one's life because embracing this belief means that we doom the poor to meaningless lives. More black men and women, people of color, and white women are falling into the ranks of the poor every day. More fall into addiction to ease the pain and shame they feel about poverty. A culture of addiction breeds violence. And ultimately their lives come to embody the nihilism that the dominant culture identifies with the poor. This nihilism exists among all classes in the United States. It is the direct consequence of the total devaluation of human life, of what happens when things become more important than people.

If we are to change both the fate of our nation and the collective lot of African Americans, we need to focus first and foremost on self-determination. We need to have a worldview grounded in the belief that one's life can have value irrespective of economic status. We need to reaffirm the primacy of community, connectedness, and sharing. Focusing more on progressive parenting that teaches black children self-love and self-esteem will ensure their attainment of well-being and the good life more than any emphasis on acquiring skills to make money. Economic self-sufficiency is important and vital. But it alone will not ensure health or fulfillment. Decolonized black folks with healthy self-esteem are more likely to succeed in any endeavor. To truly resist white supremacy and racism in all its manifestations we need to be psychologically healthy. Our movements to collectively address internalized racism in black life have failed again and again because the leaders of these movements have often not divested of their own hatred of blackness, their allegiance to color castes, their worship of whiteness.

Concurrently, we cannot heal the crisis in black life without in-corporating in our struggle for black self-determination the struggle to end sexism and male domination. Family life (committed marriages and partnerships) in diverse black communities is daily undermined by patriarchal thinking that makes acceptable male domination in the forms of violence, psychological terrorism, betrayal, and abandon-ment. Adultery, child abuse, marital rape, and date rape are all expres-sions of black male sexism. And that sexism is often condoned by black women who support and embrace patriarchal thinking. Black on black male violence is a feminist issue. Black men need feminist thinking to resist being brainwashed by white supremacist patriarchal thinking into believing that being a man is about the will to do vio-lence and coerce others.

We have seen again and again that black men and women who oppose racism often support sexism and class exploitation, that white women who are outraged by sexism help perpetuate and maintain structures of racism and white supremacy, that progressive white men who critique capitalism do not challenge sexist and racist thinking and behavior. As long as any of us support domination in any form, we keep in place the structure which upholds racism and white suprem-acy. Racism and white supremacy cannot be effectively challenged and changed in our society until all of us learn to resist domina-tion in all its forms. Loving justice means that we are willing to see the ways racism, sexism, and class exploitation are interconnected. It would serve us well to heed the warning posed by Martin Luther King when he prophetically declared in his "Beyond Vietnam" speech that we needed "a revolution of values in this society" emphasizing: "When machines and computers, profit motives and property rights are considered more important than people, the giant triplets of racism, materialism, and militarism"—and here I would add sexism— "are incapable of being conquered." Our hope lies in facing these truths and rededicating ourselves to a vision of life where freedom and justice for all is no longer a dream but the reality to be embraced if we are to survive, if the planet is to survive. It is only as we work for change that we see clearly that change can happen, that our lives can be transformed, that we can always renew our spirits and rekindle our hope.

17

Writing Beyond Race

Home is the only place where there is no race. Awakening in the morning I do not look at the image of my face in the bathroom mirror and think a black woman is washing her face. Watching that face I think about acne, looking to see if there is a new pimple. I think about all the ways acne has followed me from my teen years into this menopausal time of life where I am told by doctors "acne worsens in women with age." Acne has no race. It creeps upon the body indiscriminately—anyone can be caught. It steals beauty. Beauty is clear skin—no hurting sores, no ugly reminders that it is all illusory. Acne sufferers are constantly reminded that the body is not fixed and static. The body, like everything else, is subject to change. And yet we live in a culture that has made race a fixed reality, race that is always identified with the body. We live within the economy of the body as though there is no mind, as though the idea that is race is more a binding physical imprint. And yet it is when I am home, facing my body, that I am most free of race; it is there that my mind offers me liberation.

To move beyond race I ground myself in homeplace. In this house where I live race has no place. As soon as I walk out the door, race is waiting, like a watchful stalker ready to grab me and keep me in place, ready to remind me that slavery is not just in the past but here right now ready to entrap, to hold and bind. No wonder then that I want to spend most of my life inside, in the sanctuary of home where there are no shackles, no constant reminders that there is no place free of race.

Turning away from images produced in the culture of imperialist white supremacist capitalist patriarchy by refusing television and being selective about other media protects my emotional well-being. Concurrently, I have noticed that most folks, black, brown, or white, who do not watch any television or simply a small amount, who are conservative when it comes to consuming media, are more likely to refuse to make assumptions based on negative stereotypes. They are more likely to engage in mindful speech and action. One of the most difficult aspects of daily life in a white supremacist culture is that often the most well-meaning people, especially unenlightened white folks, will share inappropriate thoughts, or just white supremacist thinking. Even though race is not a taboo topic in today's culture, many folks are unable to talk race without perpetuating racist thoughts and actions. This will only change with education for critical consciousness that re-shapes thought and action.

More folks than ever before (doctors, mental healthcare professionals) are just beginning to talk deeply about the way in which coping daily with issues or race and racism creates stressful conditions that affect one's health. Of course, I would add that it is living in a culture of white supremacy that is often an unconsciously debilitating force diminishing the spirit. This is not new news for most black folks. From slavery to the present day, black folks have known that dealing with traumatic exploitation and oppression based on race creates life-threatening stress and the concomitant illnesses that come in its wake. Yet, given this reality, it is both amazing and disheartening that so little is written about ways we can create emotional well-being, which is central to health despite the ethos of the larger dominating culture.

One of my favorite books that not only helps me to write beyond race but to live well despite white supremacy is Norman Anderson's *Emotional Longevity: What Really Determines How Long You Live,* which was published in 2003. In his insightful chapter "Beyond Individual Achievement: Inequality and Race," he makes this point: "Nearly forty years since the landmark civil rights legislation of the 1960's, race and ethnicity are still used quite frequently by many people to determine everything....Not only do race and ethnicity shape many of our life experiences, they can be powerful predictors of longevity. Although many differences in health and longevity are evident between racial and ethnic groups, perhaps the most striking example is the health differences between blacks and whites. Compared to whites, blacks suffer higher death fate from nearly every illness including heart disease, cancer, diabetes, cirrhosis of the liver, and HIV/AIDS as well as from homicide." Norman Anderson cites the role of socioeconomic position as playing a central role in the bad health of most African Americans. He does not look at the data which shows that across class black women have similar life-threatening health issues, similar diseases.

No focus on these issues diminishes the value of his work; over all it's an awesome contribution for those of us wanting to understand how to create lives of emotional longevity and meaningful emotional well-being. Specifically, he offers six fundamental dimensions that together give us a chance to live fully and well: "biological well-being, psychological and behavioral well-being, environment and social well-being, economic well-being, existential/religious/spiritual well-being and emotional well-being." While he is willing to identify the self-diminishing role of stress and stressors in all our lives, he does not write about the particular stress of living in a culture of white supremacy, which is similar to and different from confronting everyday racism. With race and racism the assaults to the spirit may come from outside the self but white supremacy dangerously attacks the inner self if we are not critically vigilant.

Our collective inability to accurately identify spaces where white supremacy does not damage individuals and/or impinge on emotional well-being attests to its covert power. To move beyond race we must be selective about social space. Living in a predominately white community, where few adult black people reside, I often choose to isolate myself rather than engage a world outside my home where I cannot protect myself from the antics of folks who are not actively anti-racist. When I mention to white folks in the community that I have to be critically vigilant to ensure that the world around me consistently affirms my value, they are surprised. By creating an environment where systems of domination, in this case white supremacy, do not significantly diminish quality of life or emotional longevity, there is no chance that I or other nonwhite folks who make similar choices will overracialize our existence and fall prey to seeing black folks as always and only victims. Indeed, a primary goal of our critical vigilance is the refusal to be a victim.

To refuse victimization we must exercise the healing power of the mind. In his work on decolonization, Ivan Van Sertima continually insisted that both our minds and our imaginations have been colonized. This colonization of mind and imagination has been one of the primary reasons many black folks remain wedded to white supremacist thought and practice. There are so few psychological texts, self-help books, and/or mental health therapies that teach disempowered black folks of all classes how to discipline the mind. When anyone embraces victimization, they surrender control. They have given their minds over to a system of thought and practice that will keep suffering alive. When an individual sees themselves as always and only a victim, they are often beset by intense and powerful emotions. In his book *The Art of Happiness: A Handbook for Living,* the Dalai Lama teaches: "We also often add to our pain and suffering by being overly sensitive, overreacting to minor things, and sometimes taking things too personally. We tend to take small things too seriously and blow them up out of proportion, while at the same time we often remain indifferent to the really important things, those things which have profound effects on our lives and long-term consequences and implications."

Certainly, when we ponder why so many young black folk, many of whom come from affluent families where they received emotional care, have poor self-esteem and destructive habits of being, we need look no farther than the mind. When any black person embraces the notion that the "white" world is an all-powerful constant enemy, they lose the will to live fully. Let's be clear that this thought is an aspect of white supremacist thinking. Without mental programs that help black people decolonize and discipline the mind there will be continued psychological confusion and suffering. Holocaust survivors, survivors of genocidal attacks all over the world have identified the role the mind can play in allowing us to be self-actualized, to be compassionate, to find inner strength, to be peaceful. It is no accident that many citizens of our nation have looked to different spiritual paths, such as Buddhism, to teach us how to eliminate negative states of mind. Buddhism has helped me move beyond all politics of blame. It has offered a spiritual path to awakening that enables me to connect compassionately with myself and with other sentient beings.

Anderson's work, which honors the amazing legacy of his African American mother, emphasizes the power of faith and the importance of spiritual legacy. Indeed, black folks coming out of slavery into freedom found in liberation theology a way to be in the presence of a divine spirit that was liberating. Certainly, it is more than evident that as more black folks lose their spiritual foundations they experience greater hopelessness and despair. Long before cultural critics talked about race as a social construct, spirituality had already taught black folks that we were more than our bodies, more than our circumstance, and that there was a transcendent self and a divine power stronger than human will. Such beliefs helped black folks face suffering without falling into despair.

Anyone, and especially any black person seeking to move beyond race, can find in spiritual practice a way out of manmade constructions. Throughout the history of black experience in the United States, folks have given powerful testimony to the meaning of spirituality in our lives not as a path that takes us away from reality but as a path of mindful awareness that enables us to accept and cope with reality. Strong faith promotes optimism about one's own experience as well as compassion for others. When we are able to feel wholehearted empathy with everyone, we can move past all artificial distinctions separating and estranging us from one another.

This essay began with a discussion of home because where we live is the primary site of resistance in the lives of black folk and all other groups of people who are the targets of white supremacist aggression. To live the practice of anti-racism no matter the color of one's skin you must dare to make all the environments that you design and control places that maximize your well-being. While this is no simple task when so much outside of us impinges on all that happens inside, it is not impossible. Recently, I have moved to a renovated old house I call the sugar shack. The inside décor is inspired by the home of Mexican artist Frida Kahlo, which I visited a few years ago with African American artist Emma Amos. Kahlo is a fitting guardian angel of my home because she is a symbol of a woman artist, a woman of color dedicated to her work, to creating a legacy for herself despite chronic pain and the psychological hurt of betrayal.

Inside my home there is folk art from all over the world: a red Judas carved in wood that came from Guatemala, a black Jesus on the cross that came via Mexico to a Milagros import store in Tampa famous for its handmade soaps. Like all old houses that have not been properly cared for, the sugar shack has many flaws and is always in need of repair. Its imperfections remind me that we have all fallen short, that we are all flawed. Accepting and loving ourselves just the way we are is vital to our emotional longevity, to our emotional well-being. I believe that each time I open my front door, crossing the threshold to enter the sugar shack, invisible strong brown arms are reaching out to welcome me, to hold me close.

At home, in that space beyond race, I write. When I work with words, I enter a space that is beyond race. And yet it is often the writing that does not address race that has difficulty finding an audience. Early on in my work I talked of "language as a place of struggle." In the culture of imperialist white supremacist capitalist patriarchy, it is not surprising that I as a black female would need to struggle to engage in healthy self-love without embracing limiting identity politics. Living in dominator culture we are often trapped by language that imprisons us in binaries, either/or options that will not let us claim all the bits and pieces of ourselves, our hearts, especially the pieces that do not fit with neat categories. In mid-life I have had much opportunity to reflect on the way in which the over-racialization of the lives of black people/people of color often prevents us from full self-actualization and self-expression.

Unlike other historical moments where we were without voice, we now face a public culture of covert domination that seeks to limit our voice and by so doing, limit the scope of both our thought and influence. After writing and publishing more than twenty books, looking retrospectively at my writing career, at my work as a feminist theorist and cultural critic, I can see that it is the writing that moves beyond race that receives little attention. By placing me in categories that close off readership rather than expand public awareness of the holistic nature of my being, the publishing and reading public (even the most dedicated bell hooks readers) deny the complexity of my being and becoming.

While working on this essay, I notice for the first time the promotional marketing blurb for a favorite work of mine, *Remembered Rapture: The Writer At Work,* which concluded with this statement: "once again, these essays reveal bell hooks' wide-ranging intellectual scope—a universal writer addressing readers and writers everywhere." Yes. This is how I see myself, a passionate writer with many passions. And it is keeping that universal perspective in mind that inspires me to write from the various locations of self and identity that inform my life, that keep me writing beyond race.

18

The Practice of Love

In theologian Henri Nouwen's book *With Open Hands,* he includes a section on "Prayer and Revolution," which ends with the declaration:"God, give me the courage to be revolutionary ...Give me the courage to loosen myself from this world. Teach me to stand up free and to shun no criticism ...Make me free, make me poor in this world, then I will be rich in the real world, which this life is all about. God, thank you for the vision of the future, but make it fact and not just theory." In keeping with Nouwen's insistence that we move always from theory to practice, *Writing Beyond Race* is subtitled *Living Theory and Practice.* This subtitle is meant to evoke for the reader an awareness that there is an experiential practice that the forthcoming ideas and theory are meant to bring forth. Theory, then, becomes a map that if followed will guide us in the direction of liberatory terrain. This is especially true of theory that aims to heighten our awareness of the ways living in a culture of domination governed by a politics of imperialist white supremacist capitalist patriarchy impacts all our lives.

Psychotherapist Arno Gruen reminds us in his book *Betrayal of the Self* that domination, the will to exert power and control over others, is "antithetical to human nature and...causes not only the 'betrayal of the self' but of almost all that is morally and politically evil or reprehensible in the world. The quest for power and control (and the corollary tendency to overvalue abstract thought) dehumanizes us, causing internal disassociation and denying us access to such elementary human urges as love and empathy." This wounding of the psyche affects both dominator and dominated. Particularly, I want to focus on the psychic impact of white supremacist domination on the minds and imaginations of black folk. Certainly white supremacy as an ever-constant form of domination in our society demands that black people split off parts of themselves to function in a society that covertly and overtly requires its citizens to live in obedience to unspoken beliefs and habits that help maintain fictions of racial difference.

To live a life that is not in collusion with white supremacist thought and actions black folks must choose active resistance. To live as people of integrity we must remain ever critically vigilant. The *Webster* dictionary defines integrity as "the quality or state of being complete, wholeness." A simple way to understand integrity is to know that it is present when there is congruency between what we think, say, and do. All too often the politics of white supremacy and its concomitant notions of race and racism lead black people and everyone else to engage daily in habits of being that lack integrity. Think of the many white folks who say they are not racist who then proceed to consciously create lives where they have little or no contact with people who are of a different race. At a seemingly progressive college where I am sometimes in residence, a white male student openly flaunts his belief that black people are of inferior intelligence and white people superior. In the small predominately white town where I live, folks, white and black, will say they are not racist but then explain that they are against interracial marriage. Since from childhood on, we are all inundated with the thinking of white supremacy, it should not surprise anyone that black people/people of color often share with their white counterparts' irrational assumptions, beliefs, and prejudices based on stereotypical notions of racial difference.

Since all citizens of our nation are subjected to some form of indoctrination that socializes us to embrace, however unconsciously, aspects of white supremacist thought and action, however relative, we must consciously choose to acquire the necessary critical consciousness that empowers us to think and act differently, to resist. Resistance to white supremacy, to racism, requires constant critical vigilance because in every aspect of our society white supremacy is normalized. Therefore we (irrespective of racial identity) can only move beyond the prejudicial beliefs and assumptions racism offers us by applying strategies of decolonization—that is, strategies aimed at strengthening our awareness of the true reality beyond domination and providing us with an oppositional liberating worldview. We change our minds and hearts by changing our habits of thinking and being. Internalized white supremacy and racism prevent everyone from achieving emotional well-being; this is especially the case for black people who lack critical consciousness. As long as most black folks are emotionally crippled by internalized white supremacist thinking, they are trapped in split-mind enacting behaviors that reinforce patterns of racist stereotypes even as they may voice anti-racist sentiments.

Even though it is not a popular topic, given the mainstream success of some individual black folks, internalized white supremacist thinking and behavior daily assault the psyches of unaware black folks, preventing them from achieving optimal well-being. In particular, white supremacist aesthetics, especially as they pertain to body image, promote the cultivation of a diminished sense of self-worth. Black children watch television for more hours than their white counterparts. Who can know how many messages they receive in just one day communicating that black is bad and white good? A commonly accepted expression of internalized racism that most black folks passively accept is the assumption that anyone who has fair skin and females who have long straight hair have more value and worth and are more likely to succeed. Looking through all the *Jet* magazines published in 2011, it is possible to count the number of black females who have short hair and/or natural hair on two hands.

Many unaware white folks standing on the outside looking in often express the opinion that black people are too obsessed with race and racism. Yet their standpoint is merely a reflection of white privilege—one that allows them to remain in denial of the impact hardcore racist socialization has on black people. Certainly, white folks remain in control of the television media, which is easily the most accessible propagandistic mouthpiece for white supremacy. And it is even easier for unenlightened white folks to remain ignorant of the myriad ways white supremacist thinking socializes black folks to believe that race is the most important defining aspect of black identity. Hence it is almost impossible for those black folks who internalize these beliefs to simply move beyond race.

However, we can choose to live in ways that offer us a different life focus. The most vital strategy for changing anyone's fixation on race is full-on engagement with the practice of love. Enslaved religious black folks found their way to a liberation theology that affirmed their right to resist bondage and the relegation to second-class citizenship laying claim to humanizing values in the midst of dehumanization and holocaust. Contemporary black folks must work to follow their example. We must work to decolonize our minds so that we can think and act freely. All black folks who would decolonize our minds so that white supremacist thinking and action has no place in our lives must pay close attention to self-actualization. We must dare to love. We must recognize love as the transformative practice that will free our minds and bodies.

I began to write about love when I saw clearly the ways low self-esteem kept many black folks mired in self-hate. Lecturing all over the world, I found through conversations with folks who had decolonized their minds that they often began this shift because of deep feelings of love. It might be love for another person or love of justice. Significantly, it was always love that created the motivation for profound inner and outer transformation. Love was the force that empowered folks to resist domination and create new ways of living and being in the world.

Indeed, in the first book of my love trilogy, *All About Love*, I stated again and again that "anytime we do the work of love we are doing the work of ending domination." In this work I tell readers that love is a combination of five factors—care, commitment, knowledge, responsibility, and trust. Lecturing, I would tell readers to imagine that they want to bake a cake but they lack essential ingredients. Simply put, without all the essential ingredients working together they cannot achieve the desired end. The same is true of love. Without the essential ingredients working together we cannot fully engage the practice of love. All too often in our society folks equate care with love. This misunderstanding of the nature of love allows them to think that they can be loving even as they are engaged in acts of self-betrayal, even as they hurt and even abuse individuals with whom they are involved emotionally. Love and abuse are antithetical. We cannot abuse someone and insist we love them. Abuse is always about abandonment. We cannot dominate someone and insist we are being loving. And most importantly, if we are self-loving, we do not allow ourselves to be dominated. Healthy self-affirmation and self-esteem will always give us the personal strength to set appropriate boundaries.

To make self-love primary as a black person in white supremacist culture is a choice that automatically engages one in counter-hegemonic political resistance. Sadly, many black folks are unable to love because the power of internalized racism invites constant betrayal of the self. Again, when parents allow black children to consume hours and hours of television shows that both covertly and overtly carry the message that black identity is negative, they place their child at risk. Despite good intentions, they are not establishing a positive foundation for personal growth. Parents may verbally offer positive ideas about blackness but their voices carry little weight in the face of a larger media that claims to represent reality. This is just one example of the way in which black people are forced to live schizophrenic lives, always maintaining a dual consciousness.

Many of the ways in which black people are socialized to always have a split mind concern body image. Since the mainstream culture of white supremacy and the white privilege it puts in place over-determines standards of acceptable body images, of beauty, black folks may condemn racism on one hand and on the other hand be striving to meet the standards developed by a racist mindset. Recently, popular culture's focus on black female obsession with possessing long straight hair has exposed the underlying low self-esteem that more often than not fuels this obsession.

Significantly, there is no great abundance of theory that speaks to the struggle that must take place—both on the interpersonal psychological level and on a political level—for black folks to build healthy self-esteem. A core issue black people face is whether or not to act in collusion with the existing white supremacist culture or to resist by choosing to actively create an alternative worldview that upholds honest self-evaluation and positive personal growth. To be people of integrity, to not engage in endless everyday acts of self-betrayal, black folks can choose to love. That choice will automatically negate engagements with white supremacist thinking and practice. In his insightful book *Love and Betrayal,* therapist John Amodeo explains: "We live with integrity by discovering the values that are dear to us and periodically asking ourselves if we're living according to those values as best we can.... A life of integrity also asks us to question our beliefs and standpoints." To live with integrity black folks must be willing to be critically vigilant.

Clearly, when racial segregation was the norm and black people faced daily outright racist discrimination and constant harassment, it was easier for everyone to resist ideologies of white supremacy. It was only through acts of anti-racist resistance that black folks could hope to gain civil rights and access to a better life. Critical vigilance in a world of racial apartheid was needed as the circumstances black people faced were so often life threatening. When racial integration offered more ways for black folk to thrive within the existing culture of domination, that critical vigilance began to fall away. Assimilation into the existing social structure rather than counter-hegemonic resistance became the order of the day.

Racial de-segregation did not mean that the underlying philosophical structures of white supremacist thought were radically changed. In reality to maintain this system those structures became pronounced. Integration with no real change in the underlying structure of white supremacy placed black folks in positions of extreme emotional vulnerability. To work for white people, to be deemed acceptable by that dominating group, black folks were compelled to look and act in ways that did not threaten white power and privilege. This is the social reality that lays the groundwork for black folks' poor mental health. It encouraged the cultivation of a schizophrenic mindset. It is this split that Harlem Renaissance poet Paul Laurence Dunbar proclaims in his famous poem "We Wear the Mask," which begins with the lines "we wear the mask that grins and lies."

Given the psychological dilemmas black folks face in a culture of white supremacist domination, there should be an abundance of theoretical and self-help literature aimed to lay the groundwork for the building of healthy self-esteem and healthy self-love. Yet it is rare in our culture to find work that critically examines the psychological impact of self-betrayal on the psyches of black folks. When black people spend our lives wearing a mask to survive and succeed in the culture of white supremacy, we do violence to our authentic selves. We cannot know who we really are.

This split mind promotes the growth of an exaggerated focus on race and racism in black life. It creates the groundwork for the cultivation of an identity based solely on seeing oneself as always and only a victim. John Amodeo contends that we become people of integrity by moving toward wholeness "as we take the initiative to look honestly at ourselves and come to know ourselves as we really are." Becoming stuck in victim consciousness creates a paralysis of the will that inhibits personal growth. Without a foundation of healthy self-esteem we cannot become people of integrity. Amodeo reminds us that "integrity refers to a life orientation in which we are committed to becoming more self-aware and appropriately responsive to others. Rather than blaming others…we trade in our role of victim for the role of self-responsible adult who culls the learning inherent in all life experience…however unpleasant this may be." Challenging and eliminating an ethos of victimhood is essential for black self-determination and self-actualization. Choosing to love is one way we resist any notion of being a victim. Actively loving, one refuses victim consciousness. The practice of love always demands of us constant recognition of our own essential worth and value.

To value ourselves rightly we are called to move beyond race. We are called to recognize that ethnicity, that skin color, are but one fragment of a holistic identity. To overemphasize or dwell pathologically on this one fragment blocks self-awareness and self-understanding. To know ourselves beyond race, beyond the tenets of white supremacist logic, we must always embrace the wholeness that is the necessary foundation if we are to live with integrity.

By embracing the transformative power of love we accept the fullness of our humanity, which then allows us to recognize the humanity of others. Within that recognition we can engage a practice of loving kindness, forgiveness, and compassion. In *With Open Hands,* Henri Nouwen shares that "compassion is daring to acknowledge our mutual destiny so that we might move forward all together." Mutuality is formed through a shared understanding of what it means to love.

To engage the practice of love is to oppose domination in all its forms. To love will necessarily take us beyond race, beyond all categories that aim to limit and confine the human spirit. Domination will never end as long as we are all taught to devalue love. In her book *The Age of Miracles,* visionary thinker Marianne Williamson urges us to choose to love. She shares this insight: "Miracles occur naturally in the presence of love. In our natural states we are miracle workers because love is who we are. Talk about personal transformation—the journey from fear to love is not a narcissistic exercise ... it's the most necessary component to our re-creating human society and affecting the course of history." To fully embrace the transformative power of love, we would need to have the revolution of values Martin Luther King called for before his untimely demise.

If we were to gather all the cultural criticism and critical theory on the subject of white supremacy, whiteness, race, and racism, in this huge body of work, we would find little or no focus on love. Yet all our deconstructive explanatory theory is meaningless if it is not rooted in the recognition that the most fundamental challenge to domination is the choice to love. Love as a way of life makes it possible for us all to live humanely within a culture of domination as we work for change. The radical nature of love is that it is profoundly democratic. Irrespective of our status and station in life we can choose love; we can choose to leave dominator thinking behind.

Love moves us beyond categories and therein lies its power to liberate. Free to love, we are free to be our authentic selves. We are free to take the path that leads us away from domination toward new lives of optimal well-being. We are free to think, to write, to dream, to live beyond race.